Driven by Nis

Driven by Nissan?

A critical guide to the new
management techniques

Dave Beale

Lawrence & Wishart
London

Lawrence and Wishart Limited
144a Old South Lambeth Road
London SW8 1XX

First published 1994
Copyright © Dave Beale 1994

Text design and typesetting by Jan Brown Designs, London
Printed and bound in Great Britain by Redwood Books, Trowbridge

Contents

Acknowledgements

This book has been a long time in the making, and many individuals and organisations have assisted me along the way. I suspect that many people who have helped me were not fully aware at the time of the value of their assistance. So to put the record straight...

Particular thanks to John Pemberton, former trade union studies tutor at Preston College and currently manager of Preston and District Unemployed Centre, for the countless discussions, comments, ideas and information about new management techniques and possible trade union responses, since our mutual interest in the subject emerged in 1985. Thanks to Dave Barnes, trade union studies tutor at Blackpool and Fylde College, for his numerous ideas and information, particularly with regard to the chapter on labour flexibility; to Lynne Humphrey, researcher at the Manchester Employment Research Group, for her ideas, commitment and encouragement in this project, and for the immense volume of work she has carried out for the Manchester Employment Research Group, which has greatly assisted me.

The Manchester Employment Research Group, established in 1979 as the Manchester Engineering Research Group and known as MERG, is a small but influential organisation concerned with research and the provision of collective bargaining information to the trade union movement primarily in the North West. New management techniques and possible trade union responses have been a central part of its work in recent years. Therefore, I hope that those trade unionists with whom this book finds favour will attribute to the Manchester Employment Research Group the credit and wider recognition it so deserves, and will provide the financial support it urgently needs to continue its work.

Thanks also to the following: Ian Brown, then Trade Union and Industrial Liaison Officer and currently Economic Development Officer for Manchester City Council, for his encouragement and ideas at the early stages of this project; the Management Committee of the Manchester

Employment Research Group for its interest and encouragement; No.30 (Preston) District Committee of the Confederation of Shipbuilding and Engineering Unions for its endorsement of the Employers' New Offensive Project Group from which this book emerged; Preston Trades Union Council for its continuing interest in the project; the activists of the North West Coast district of MSF, for their interest, encouragement, provision of useful information, and for opportunities to test out some of my ideas on the subject in debate with them; and North West Water Unison branch officers for allowing me to speak and participate in their pioneering weekend school on the subject of new management techniques.

Thanks to shop stewards and union representatives throughout Central Lancashire, and sometimes further afield, with whom I have discussed the nature, problems and issues of new management techniques and possible union responses and strategies on many trade union courses for which I have been a tutor, and at many union meetings and union schools on the subject to which I have been invited. Without the interest, ideas, criticisms and willingness of these shop stewards to share their experience, this book would simply not have happened; they convinced me of the need for a critical guide to new management techniques in the first place, and it is to those trade union activists that this book is dedicated. In particular, thanks to shop stewards and union representatives at the following workplaces in the Preston area: British Aerospace, Leyland Trucks and former Leyland Daf companies, GEC Alsthom, Royal Mail, Farington Components (Volvo Group), Baxi Partnership, Rockwell Graphic Systems, Royal Ordnance, Preston Bus, Dairy Crest and British Nuclear Fuels.

Thanks to Sally Davison of Lawrence and Wishart for pointing me in the right direction when I was clueless about the technicalities of publishing. Thanks to Crissie Laugesen and to my parents and family for their great encouragement and interest. And not least to my daughter Nicola. In spite of the cynics, the pundits and all the obstacles in the way of a powerful, international trade union movement, may the cause of organised labour be every bit as relevant to her life as it has been to mine.

Introduction

New management techniques are an important issue for industrial relations in the UK in the 1990s. In the political and economic climate of the 1980s they emerged as a pioneering combination of new management initiatives, particularly in the car and consumer electronics industries. Nissan and the subsequent Japanese investment projects in the car industry received extensive media attention.

Single union no-strike agreements, large greenfield sites in areas of high unemployment, extensive labour flexibility and the end of restrictive working practices, multi-skilling, just-in-time production, total quality and zero defects, employee involvement and visions of management rolling up their sleeves were the images of the new industrial relations which the media conjured up for public consumption.

With significant encouragement from numerous management consultants, the Department of Trade and Industry, and Japanese and US companies in the UK, employers in a wide range of industries realised that the introduction of new management techniques was the thing to do (even if some of them were not entirely sure why). The chemical industry pioneered many of the 'blockbuster' agreements on labour flexibility. Non-manufacturing sectors such as the retail trade realised the advantages of just-in-time and customer-orientated quality systems. The public sector began to link new management techniques to the challenge of public spending cuts and the threat of privatisation. In short, a process of diffusion of new management techniques throughout almost all sectors of employment began in the 1980s, and developed apace in the 1990s.

In turn, this process has come to pose a challenge of major proportions to both trade unions and management in the UK. Do unions recognise the challenge to their power, authority and independence? What could trade unions do to meet this challenge effectively? Have management in the

UK the ability to meet the challenge posed?

The intention of this book is to provide a clear guide to the nature of the new management techniques, and in doing so to begin to answer these important questions. With the help of a range of examples and illustrations, it aims to explain how the new management techniques operate in the workplace. It aims to explain the management objectives behind the techniques, as well as some of the historical origins and the national and international factors which are driving them. The book is a critical guide to the issues, and therefore there is an emphasis on the trade union implications and possible union response to the techniques. The book aims to be useful to practitioners of industrial relations, particularly to trade unionists who are facing these issues in their workplace. In addition, it should prove to be a useful guide for students of industrial relations.

The sub-title new management techniques is perhaps not as accurate as it might be. It has been adopted in the book's title because it is the most common term used by industrial relations practitioners. There is some justification in the argument that some of the new management techniques are not entirely new. Management initiatives to secure increased labour flexibility, particularly the use of temporary and part-time labour, sub-contracting and less restrictive working practices, are not new in themselves. Neither are some of the employee involvement initiatives, such as the team-building methods and philosophies. However, in the way in which these initiatives fit together as part of an integrated management programme, particularly as exemplified by Nissan-style workplaces, they are new.

The word 'initiatives' is more accurate than the word 'techniques' since the latter suggests the use of new management skills and methods alone, rather than a combination of these with new management philosophies. For example, just-in-time and continuous improvement are more accurately described as new management philosophies, with accompanying tools and techniques to ensure their success. The term 'initiatives' is used more frequently in the text than the the the term 'techniques' for this reason. Where there is reference to 'techniques', the word is used loosely. 'New management techniques' is used in the book's title simply because, while less accurate, it is in common usage in the workplace.

Chapter One sets the context for the emergence of the new initiatives, and in doing so outlines the national and international driving forces behind them. Chapter Two deals with the question of just-in-time philosophy, and the related question of continuous improvement. Chapter

Three assesses the concept of the flexible firm, and identifies three useful categories of labour flexibility. Chapter Four considers the important human resource management issue of employee involvement, the underlying principles and the wide range of employee involvement methods and techniques. Single union no-strike deals, total quality initiatives and teamworking are the basis of Chapter Five. The two concluding chapters of the book attempt to tie together the detailed issues considered in chapters two to five. Chapter Six does this through a consideration of the implications for new management initiatives in the UK of economic, political and international trends; Chapter Seven is a general assessment and comment on both management and trade union weaknesses in respect of the new management initiatives, and the potential for an effective response to new management initiatives by unions in the UK.

Since completion of chapters one to seven, certain new management initiatives in the public sector may have gained greater prominence than the text sometimes suggests. In particular, the challenge of performance indicators and performance-related pay has become a critical issue for many public sector workers who had traditionally considered such matters inapplicable to them because of the nature of their work. Such performance questions in the public sector are commonly related to staff appraisal schemes, and cannot be divorced from total quality initiatives, financial devolution, the extension of 'personal' contracts, the break-up of large public sector organisations into smaller units, public spending cuts, market testing and privatisation. Performance management has become a key concept. Whilst this book does not ignore public sector issues, it is orientated towards the private, industrial and union organised sector. There may well be a place for future separate volumes which focus on new management initiatives not only in the public sector, but also in the private service sector of employment. However, the following pages aim to provide a useful start as a critical guide to the current issues.

Before proceeding to Chapter One the reader might find the following brief explanation of key terms helpful.

Just-in-time methods bring about minimum levels of stock at all stages of the production process. Production is much more closely related to fluctuations in customer demand. Such a system is intended to create a series of repercussions which result in radical changes to working practices and workplace philosophy. The closer to 'zero inventory' that a workplace gets, the more that problems in the production process are forced to the surface, creating a situation in which it becomes very difficult for workers to avoid lasting solutions to them. Total quality management initiatives are a necessary ingredient, and increased flexibility of labour, employee involvement and teamworking generally play an important role in establishing a developed system. Employers can make major financial savings from just-in-time.

Labour flexibility is a term often used to refer to several rather different types of labour practices. A useful way of resolving common confusion about its precise meaning is to distinguish between numerical labour flexibility (temporary, part-time and casual labour), functional flexibility (the breakdown of demarcation between different skills and/or between skilled, semi-skilled and unskilled labour) and temporal flexibility (flexibility regarding working time, such as averaged and annualised hours agreements, more flexible shift arrangements and flexitime).

Employee involvement refers to a range of techniques which include team briefings, attitude surveys, video presentations, employers' newspapers, quality circles and related problem-solving groups, employee share-ownership plans, profit-sharing schemes, profit-related pay, works councils and other workplace consultative committees and structures. Employee involvement is about improving workplace communication, loyalty to the company, increased awareness of the organisation's needs and better use of employees' 'shopfloor' expertise.

Total quality management or TQM is a term used in a confusing variety of ways. Perhaps one of the most useful approaches is to see it as a broad concept which encompasses various stages of quality assurance through which companies and organisations might progress. Seen like this TQM can refer to anything from BS 5750, through to the concept of every employee having responsibility for quality and getting things 'right first time', to concepts of value which incorporate major improvements in quality simultaneously with vigorously competitive pricing strategies.

Teamworking is a system usually applied to manual workers in industrial workplaces. It refers to the establishment of teams of between approximately ten and twenty, and provides workers with a much greater level of autonomy within the team with regard to how their work is organised. Common outcomes of teamworking are to create greater levels of functional labour flexibility within the team, to promote employee involvement and total quality initiatives, to change radically supervisory roles and to act as an important vehicle for the introduction of just-in-time.

Chapter 1

Conservative government, Japanese industry and new management techniques

The aim of this first chapter is to try to explain how and why the new management techniques and initiatives associated with just-in-time production, labour flexibility, employee involvement, single union deals, total quality and teamworking have emerged as important items on the agenda of industrial relations in the UK since the early 1980s.

Conservative government: the context

Many of these new management methods have their *origins* in the USA, and were *developed* by Japanese industry, primarily in motor vehicles and electronics. Just-in-time itself, however, both originated and was developed in Japan. (The second part of this chapter provides the evidence to support these points.) US and Japanese multinationals have a greater presence in the UK than any other European country, and the Single European Market has increased the speed of intensification of international competition both within the European Union and outside it. These factors are all important in explaining the appearance of just-in-time production, labour flexibility packages, employee involvement programmes, single union deals, total quality initiatives and teamworking as key items on the agenda of UK industrial relations in the 1980s and 90s. But what about the policy of Conservative governments since 1979? Has Conservative policy played an important part in encouraging UK management to take these new management initiatives? (Or would they have happened in any case?) The first part of this chapter provides a brief review of the main changes relevant to industrial relations brought about by Conservative government policy since 1979, and how these might be related to the various new management initiatives.

Conservative economic policy

Conservative economic policy has had several dimensions to it. The attack on inflation through monetarist policy in the early period of Conservative government coincided with a dramatic and sudden rise in unemployment and a serious economic recession within months of the Conservatives coming to power in 1979. The manufacturing sector suffered the worst, with government policy providing encouragement to finance capital and the private service sector. There was an economic recovery after 1981, but this did not make itself felt in terms of any great decline in unemployment. The main expansion in numbers of jobs was in the private service and finance sectors. In the case of the former, these were predominantly temporary and part-time. They were in sectors with traditionally weak trade union organisation, if any at all, with resultant poor wages and conditions. This restructuring of the economy which took place also took on a geographical dimension; it played an important part in the further development of a North-South divide in the UK.

Two further points need to be made about the unemployment figures since 1979. First they need to be seen in perspective. For the best part of twenty five years the promise of the Beveridge Report to hold unemployment below 3 per cent was kept, but in the late 1960s things began to change and unemployment had drifted upwards to 5 per cent by 1976. Following Thatcher's election victory of 1979, the figures doubled in three years, and exceeded 12 per cent by the mid-1980s. By the late 1980s the figures declined to some degree, but still retained a level of four to five times that of twenty years earlier.[1]

The second point is that the method for calculating unemployment figures has been amended more than thirty times since the Conservatives came to power.[2]

People in employment in Great Britain, 1981-84	
Industry	Change in 000s
Metal goods, engineering and vehicles	− 429
Other manufacturing	− 185
Distribution, hotels, catering, repairs	+ 95
Banking, finance, insurance, business services, etc	+ 260
Other services	+ 151
Whole economy	− 463
Source: Census of Employment 1984 [3]	

At various stages in the period of Conservative government since 1979, high interest rates have been an important issue because of the problems caused particularly for business and home-owners by the high cost of borrowing money. By autumn 1990, this had coincided with evidence of recession in the UK economy, as well as the culmination of the conflict between UK government policy and that of European Community partners with the resignation of Thatcher.[4] Another important debate concerns the nature of recovery from economic recession in the UK.

There is evidence to suggest that the 1979-81 recession was a significant factor in encouraging companies to go for 'blockbuster' agreements on labour flexibility. The evidence (outlined in chapter three) suggests that there was a significant increase in extensive agreements, often enabling agreements, which aimed to break down demarcation between jobs on the shopfloor and introduced degrees of functional flexibility.

It would not be surprising if economic recession combined with high interest rates were factors in encouraging the introduction of just-in-time production, since the latter entails the radical reduction of stock levels and can release significant amounts of money in the process. Whether this occurred in pioneering companies in 1979-81 is unclear. It is debatable whether UK management at that time was sufficiently conversant with the ideas of just-in-time to exploit the possibilities. An interesting question is whether the recession which began in 1990 will prove to have been significant in encouraging a more widespread introduction of just-in-time in the UK. The number of strikes in the UK has declined significantly since 1979 and the role of high unemployment in bringing this about is difficult to dispute. And a weakness of just-in-time is that it is vulnerable to strike action because of low stock levels. This therefore suggests the possibility that employers have felt more confident about introducing just-in-time because of the reduced likelihood of strikes.

As for the restructuring of the economy which has taken place, the expansion of the private service sector has meant a growth of part-time, temporary and casual labour. Such labour is part of what is meant by numerical flexibility. There are often considerable cost advantages for employers in the use of such labour, in terms of National Insurance costs, occupational pension contributions, sick pay, employment protection rights and the general ease of hiring and firing.

Anti-union legislation since 1979

The Conservative governments since 1979 have introduced an extensive

7

programme of legislation aimed to reduce the power of trade unions. This has coincided with the widespread repeal since 1979 of the employment protection legislation introduced by the 1974-79 Labour government.

The Conservatives' anti-union legislation has been built around a series of statutes: the Employment Act 1980, the Employment Act 1982, the Trade Union Act 1984, the Employment Act 1988, the Employment Act 1990 and the 1993 Trade Union Reform and Employment Rights Act. To this list must be added the 1986 Wages Act and the 1989 Employment Act; the former opened the way for cashless pay with wages being paid directly into workers' bank accounts, and the latter removed restrictions on the employment of young people and women. The 1980, 82, 84, 88, and 1990 Acts dealt with three main areas: the 'right' to take and organise industrial action, internal union affairs and the closed shop.

i. Unlike the position in a number of European countries (France, Spain and Italy, for example), *there has never been a legal right to strike in the UK.* Instead, in the wake of the infamous Taff Vale case, the 1906 Trades Disputes Act gave trade unions *immunity* from legal action which could arise as a result of 'civil wrongs' which occur when unions organise strike action. These immunities are the alternative in the UK to a legal right to strike. *Fundamental to the Conservatives anti-union laws has been an ever-increasing restriction of trade unions' entitlement to immunity;* trade unions have to meet a long list of conditions before they are immune to legal action by employers when they take industrial action. Most forms of sympathy action (renamed secondary action by the Conservatives) were made unlawful by the 1982 Act. The 1984 Trade Union Act introduced a requirement for ballots before industrial action. There are now circumstances in which unions can be sued by third parties and union members in the event of unlawful industrial action. Employers have greater legal freedom to sack strikers. Picketing has to be limited to a worker's own place of work, and some state benefits have been withdrawn from strikers' dependants.

ii. The 1984 Trade Union Act was a milestone in legal interference in internal union affairs, introducing clauses which overrode some sections of union rulebooks. It introduced a requirement for unions to hold periodic ballots for political funds. The unions managed to turn this part of the legislation to their advantage, with all those with political funds maintaining their right to hold them, with impressive ballot results. A significant number of unions without political funds balloted successfully for them. More of a problem for unions were the requirements to hold secret ballots for the elections to national executive committees, supplemented by additional requirements under the 1988 Employment Act. Attempts by unions to discipline members for ignoring strike votes (even if called within the legal restrictions) have been made unlawful. There are new complex rules for keeping union accounts, and unions cannot pay members' legal costs and fines for strike offences.

iii. The closed shop, whilst still not unlawful as such, has had a number of legal restrictions placed upon it by the 1982, 88 and 90 Employment Acts. Industrial action in defence of a closed shop is unlawful. Compensation is available for non-union members who are sacked, and the 1990 Act provides a right not to be refused work on the grounds of either union membership or non-union membership.

iv. The Conservative governments since 1979 have made considerable efforts to eradicate the effect on industrial relations of the employment protection legislation of the 1970s. A series of limitations has been introduced on women workers' rights to return to their employment after maternity. Workers are required to have two years in the same employment before they are entitled to receive reasons for dismissal and to pursue an industrial tribunal claim. They have no right to minimal compensation if they win their tribunal case, and they may have to pay a deposit to the tribunal. Workers in small companies are hit in particular, with no right to know the disciplinary procedures, and with women workers losing all rights to return to employment after maternity.

Perhaps the most clear-cut example of Conservative employment legislation acting to encourage the new management initiatives is the repeal of employment protection rights and the increased numerical flexibility of labour this has allowed employers.

There can be little doubt that this amounts to the most ambitious attempt *through law* to restrict trade union power since the Taff Vale case in 1901. The trade union movement is certainly bruised as a result, but there has to be serious doubt about whether the changes in the law since 1979 have brought about any permanent changes to the basic nature of trade unionism in the UK.[5]

On another front, at the heart of much Conservative anti-union legislation from 1984 onwards has been the promotion of the 'freedom of the individual'. Much of this has exploited trade unions' failure to address adequately the problem of low levels of membership participation in union affairs. The freedom of the individual is an important part of the philosophy behind the legal requirements for secret ballots for union elections, industrial action and political funds, restrictions on the closed shop and various 'rights of redress' bestowed on union members. These legal measures are part of a broader ideological message conveyed by Conservative governments since 1979, one which argues for freedom through individualism and against the restraints of collectivism which is epitomised by trade union organisation. The measures which the Conservatives have introduced to encourage the growth of individualism include many which aimed to undermine the loyalty of workers to their union. Central to the new employee involvement methods is the aim of replacing union loyalty with company loyalty, whether it be through team briefings, quality circles, attitude surveys or profit-sharing schemes. It seems feasible to argue that the Conservative legislation portrayed as restoring power to individual union members has encouraged management to introduce employee involvement.

It is likely that the Conservative programme of anti-union legislation has built up the confidence of employers to introduce change at the workplace in terms of just-in-time, labour flexibility, employee involvement, total quality and teamworking. Unemployment, however, may have been more important in building the confidence of employers to introduce such changes.

Major disputes in the 1980s

In reviewing UK industrial relations in the 1980s, it is difficult to ignore certain major disputes which emerged as aggressive attempts by employers to destroy effective trade unionism at their company or organisation. The *Stockport Messenger* dispute at Eddie Shah's site at Warrington, the miners' strike, the News International dispute at Wapping, the ban on trade union rights at GCHQ and the seafarers' dispute with P&O in the wake of the Zeebrugge disaster, are the main ones which come to mind. All these ended in defeats of varying degrees for the trade unions. However, to focus purely on these disputes is probably misleading. As MacInnes has argued, the traffic was not all one way, and the trade unions have not been without some victories.[6] He has provided some important evidence to support this argument.

MacInnes argues that the cases where the employers have gone on the offensive have fallen into two main categories: those where the government has been the ultimate employer, and those in certain special sectors, namely Fleet Street printing, the car industry, coal and steel.[7] In the case of the former, the government was prepared to underwrite the bill for the cost of certain major confrontations with the trade unions. The obvious example of this was, of course, the miners' strike. For public sector employers to engage trade unions in the coal industry, steel and the civil service in such set-piece battles was not really a feasible option for the employers without sustentation from potentially limitless public funds.[8] In the second category (Fleet Street, car plants, coal and steel) workers were in a particularly weak bargaining position because of high unsold stock levels and/or low levels of demand. Either employers wanted to close large sections of their operation or a readily substitutable workforce was available. Coal and steel, of course, fall into the first *and* second categories.

It would be hard to deny that these disputes have had an important effect in undermining the confidence of most trade unionists to embark upon major strike action at most levels and in most sectors of the economy. To argue that they are evidence of the destruction of trade union power in the UK is quite another point. Trade union power is not an easy thing to measure. However, if the confidence of many trade unionists has been undermined by these defeats, then, correspondingly, the confidence of employers to take radical initiatives at the workplace has been enhanced. Defeats for trade unionism in these major disputes have helped to create a climate in the UK in which employers feel much more confident to take all sorts of initiatives – including just-in-time, labour flexibility, employee involvement, total quality and teamworking initiatives – which undermine and cut across trade union organisation and authority at the workplace.

Privatisation

Privatisation and on-going public spending cuts have created an important environment in which the development of new management initiatives and techniques in the UK have flourished.

Since 1979 nationalised industries and public corporations have been a major target of privatisation such that the total workforce employed by them fell from over two million to 844,000 in the first ten years alone.[9] Amongst its many implications, such privatisation has been a means for advocating the concept of the 'share-owning democracy', with government campaigns aimed at encouraging the general public to buy shares in the newly privatised industries. This is another expression of the ideology of the Conservative right, intended to promote the culture of individualism as opposed to the collectivist ideology of the trade union movement. It shares common ground with much Conservative anti-union legislation, aimed to encourage individualist attitudes and culture. It also shares common ground with employee involvement initiatives of management, intended to encourage a new workplace culture built around individualist attitudes and a concern for company problems at the expense of union loyalty.

Compulsory competitive tendering in the National Health Service and local government has been a rather different but equally important form of privatisation. Competitive tendering means that in-house tenders can be submitted, and may win the contract, but they must compete commercially with outside tenders which are also invited. The method was introduced in 1983 with a government circular ordering health authorities to put laundry, catering and cleaning services through a competitive tendering process. Largely because of the use of 'loss leader' bids private contractors took 74 per cent of all contracts by the end of the first year. However, the position was to reverse with 77 per cent of contracts being won by in-house tenders by 1989.[10]

Central to the operation of most private companies which have won contracts has been extensive numerical flexibility in the form of part-time, temporary and casual labour. This has often meant that they have been able to undercut in-house tenders, but not always able to meet the quality of service requirements of tender specifications. A convincing explanation for the high proportion of contracts won *in-house* since the late 1980s is that health authorities and local councils have become increasingly sceptical of private contractors' ability to perform the work according to contract, and that in-house services have taken extensive initiatives on two fronts.

The first of these has enabled in-house services to cut costs and compete more effectively – by increased productivity through greater workloads and increased employee performance, the increased use of part-time, temporary and other forms of casual labour, increased break down of demarcation between jobs, job losses, and deterioration in pay and conditions. Compulsory competitive tendering has thus brought both numerical and functional flexibility of labour prominently onto the agenda of in-house provision of public services. On a second front, a determination to ensure that tender specifications were met conveniently coincided with the increasing adoption of total quality methods in the public service sector, and probably played a significant part in reinforcing such quality initiatives.

During the 1980s compulsory competitive tendering was extended to a wide range of NHS services, and the 1988 Local Government Act extended it to local authority services. The effects on local authority services in terms of the introduction of new management initiatives have been essentially the same as for the NHS, except that local authorities were able to learn from the NHS experiences of the early 1980s.

However, by 1992 there were signs that the Conservatives' compulsory competitive tendering strategy was running into difficulty. This was brought about by the legal challenge by public sector unions which suggested that the government had failed to meet its legal obligation to extend the EC 1977 Acquired Rights Directive to the public sector. The government's interpretation of the Acquired Rights Directive was set out in UK law in the Transfer of Undertakings (Protection of Employment) Regulations 1981. The Acquired Rights Directive means that employees covered by it are entitled to have all their contractual rights fully protected in the event of a take-over by another employer, or of some other form of transfer of undertakings to another employer. The underlying assumption of the government programme of compulsory competitive tendering since the mid 1980s was that these employee legal rights did not apply to the public sector. As a result of the legal challenges made by public sector unions in 1992 and 1993 this ceased to be a safe assumption. Therefore, these legal developments have significantly inhibited private contractors from submitting tenders based on working conditions, and a degree of labour flexibility, which is essentially different from that of the in-house service with which they are competing. In other words, it could be in-house services rather than private contractors which in future establish the benchmark in terms of labour flexibility initiatives.

In the case of passenger transport, the 1985 Transport Act enforced widespread deregulation as a means of privatisation of bus services in the UK. This Act abolished road service licensing. Its intention was to dismantle the planned network of bus services run by local authorities and to give private operators the freedom to operate buses with minimal legal restriction. The consequences in terms of redundancies and pay cuts apart, the new possibilities for employers for more extensive numerical and temporal flexibility of labour have been significant. Employers are attempting to impose longer hours, shorter holidays and more extensive shift systems on transport workers, with the replacement of full-time drivers with part-timers in some parts of the country.[11]

Bus service deregulation has meant that over 50 publicly-owned bus operations, owned by district councils and passenger transport executives in the metropolitan areas, had to be set up as limited companies, which in turn could then be sold off. Several of these have since been established as employee share ownership plans (ESOPs). Such forms of ownership can open up a wide range of possibilities in terms of human resource management and employee involvement initiatives. These initiatives may undermine trade union independence, particularly in situations in which the ESOP is weighted in favour of a management buy-out.

Privatisation in the public service sector cannot be separated from the on-going programme of cuts, and the combined effect of the two certainly seems to be significant in bringing to the public sector another set of new management initiatives: attempts to introduce total quality management of one form or another. Financial restraints and spending pressures throughout the public service sector means that 'value for money' questions are likely to rise to the top of the agenda, with public sector management desperate to try to retain public confidence. This increased concern for users of public services is directly related to the entrepreneurial climate created by the attempts to introduce competition – between local hospitals in the NHS, and between schools, between colleges, and between universities in the education sectors. However, this is not to suggest that such a relationship is inevitable, or that Conservative ideologists have some kind of monopoly on the desire for value for money with regard to public services. It is also significant that total quality initiatives in the public service sector are implicit in the Citizen's Charter concept.

All these developments concerning privatisation and cuts open up another possible initiative by public service sector management. It is feasible that the philosophy of just-in-time could be applied to such non-manufacturing sectors, with users (whether they be patients, passengers, students or clients), or the services provided to them perceived as commodities.

The Citizen's Charter

There are links between the Citizen's Charter and total quality, public spending cuts, privatisation and market-testing initiatives, which demonstrate that the former is an important ingredient of new management initiatives in the 1990s. The Citizen's Charter concept has been applied in various ways, and is decreasingly referred to by its original name. The introduction of the Citizen's Charter had several political purposes. It appears to have been an attempt to answer the backlash of critical public opinion as a result of severe public spending cuts, not least in the National Health Service. It promised to provide the 'customers' of public services with a greater say in how services are run, which may appear to be an extension of democracy, and it forces those who work in public services to pay greater heed to what 'customers' want (a parallel with just-in-time and total quality philosophies in manufacturing).

However, the Citizen's Charter, especially when translated into its more specific forms, such as the national Patient's Charter, or the Patient's Charter for a particular district health authority, established standards for the workforce to meet as a means of ensuring the quality of the service. The charters do not refer explicitly to performance indicators, but this is how these quality standards can be perceived; neither do the charters refer to the need for improvement in productivity, but this seems to be central to their purpose. The Training and Enterprise Councils keenly promoted the Investors in People initiative. This raises the question of the use of standards as tools for the development of total quality management. The Investors in People initiative shares a common rationale with the Citizen's Charter.

The Citizen's Charter and government concepts of total quality management are tools for attempting to achieve more for a lot less in the public services, and encouraging disunity between the workforce and the public on the issue of cuts. Public sector trade unions are likely to face a very serious challenge from the development of such new management initiatives unless they develop, publicise and campaign for the implementation of alternative concepts of both quality and public accountability for the public services.

Individualism versus trade unionism

Protecting and advancing the 'rights of the individual' have been central to Conservative ideology, particularly since 1979. Thatcherite individualism, however, has gone beyond the question of 'rights'. In industrial relations it has expressed itself through a range of initiatives and policies which point towards a relationship between management and workers as individuals. Such a concept is of course directly in conflict with the traditional collectivist principles at the heart of trade unionism.

In the public sector the Conservatives have often attempted to disrupt, or sometimes abolish, the negotiating rights of trade unions at a national level. The 1987 Teachers' Pay and Conditions Act abolished national negotiating rights for school teachers. The 1988 Education Reform Act, the 1992 Further and Higher Education Act and the 1990 National Health Service and Community Care Act have aimed to create a system of private enterprise style competition at a local level, and this has opened up possibilities for the eventual substitution of national bargaining on pay and conditions by plant level bargaining in the further education and health service sectors. The subversion of national collective bargaining has occurred elsewhere in the public sector, including attempts to emphasise regional variations in pay.

An important development in recent years has been the growth of personalised payment systems, another part of the process which is undermining the power of collective bargaining to negotiate the rate for the job. An extreme example of this is the growth in numbers of employees covered by individually negotiated contracts of employment, no longer a practice exclusive to senior management in the private sector. Other examples are performance-related pay and merit pay. With associated assessment and appraisal systems, they have been an issue initially for senior and middle management, but have become an increasingly common issue for non-managerial staff grades. Public spending cuts have put performance-related pay onto the agenda of the public service sector, not least in education and the civil service. However, the system has its critics amongst management as well as the unions, since there are doubts about its effectiveness as an effective tool for employee motivation.

There are some limitations in seeing these trends purely in terms of collectivist and individualist views of the workplace. Atomisation, the reduction of something to small pieces, is perhaps a more useful term than individualism. This concept broadens the perspective on this issue, to encompass not only the termination of collective bargaining by government and employers, and the direct promotion of individualism in the workplace, but also the dismantling of the public sector carried out by successive Conservative governments. The dismantling of the public sector, whether resulting in privatisation itself, or in increasingly isolated units of a retained but reduced public sector dominated by market forces and business philosophy, has considerable significance for the introduction of new management initiatives and techniques.

A complex process of dismantling and devolution has been taking place in the NHS, education and the civil service. This has shown itself in various forms, including 'opting out' arrangements for hospitals, schools and further education colleges, local management of schools, and financial devolution.

'Opting out' and 'trust status' first became an issue in 1988 when the Education Reform Act allowed schools to 'opt out' of local education authorities. The 1992 Further and Higher Education Act went beyond this and *compelled* further education colleges to operate independently of local education authorities. The 1990 National Health Service and Community Care Act allowed hospitals to 'opt out' of district health authority control and set up self-governing independent trusts. These initiatives can be seen as part of an on-going programme aimed to establish a system based on a large number of small public sector units, isolated from each other, with democratic links with local communities severed, and much closer co-ordination and control by central government through financial mechanisms. In due course, if these circumstances prevail, workers may begin to have a lesser identification with their union because of growing obstacles to its effective operation, and a lesser identification with a national concept of their particular public service or their profession. They may begin to identify more with the specific business objectives of their own hospital, school or college, and with the markets for their new business unit and with customers rather than users. The significance of this for new management techniques is considerable, since it amounts to a very important cultural shift towards effective employee involvement at the expense of trade unionism and collective consciousness.

The dismantling of the Civil Service, linked to market testing and the promotion of business culture, may have similar implications for employee involvement. Since 1988 the Civil Service has seen a division between policy-making and administrative sectors, with the latter being split up into an ever increasing number of separate agencies.[12] With the full fifty four administrative sectors established as agencies this amounts to 193,000 staff or 34 per cent of the Civil Service.[13]

Financial devolution in education, the NHS and the civil service may also encourage employee involvement. Such devolution of budgets gives the appearance of greater control for local management. Workers in private industry have been familiar with the methods of localised cost centres for a long time. They have also been important in the privatisation of nationalised industries, and their break-up into more profitable and less profitable parts, in order to identify which parts will make the most lucrative sale. The widespread introduction of financial devolution in the public sector is related to employee involvement strategies in that it potentially encourages increased identity of employees with the organisation's financial concerns and needs. Financial devolution may also encourage a cultural devolution, in that it may force changes to management style and perspectives, and the adoption of a more open form of management, with an increasing abandonment of traditional authoritarian management methods.

Changes in trade union membership, structure and policy

Various sections of this book discuss how trade unions might and could respond to the challenge of new management initiatives and techniques. To make a balanced assessment of possible trade union responses, certain contextual factors in terms of changes to union membership, structure and general approaches to union policy need to be taken into account. The following is a brief review of the factors which are considered relevant in this respect.

The history of total trade union membership (TUC affiliated) in the UK since the late 1960s is characterised by a marked increase until 1979, followed by an equally marked decline continuing into the 1990s. TUC-affiliated membership grew from 8.7 million in 1968 to 9.4 million in 1970 and 12.1 million in 1979, declining to 9.9 million in 1985 and about 7.6 million in 1994. Non-TUC affiliated trade union membership has remained in the 1 to 1.5 million range (this does include some organisations which many people would not recognise as trade unions but which are recognised as such by the Certification Officer in accordance with the legal definition of a trade union). The figures for density of trade union membership (actual membership as a percentage of potential membership, including the unemployed but excluding the armed forces) show a similar pattern: TUC-affiliated membership density was 38 per cent in 1968, 50 per cent in 1979 and 38 per cent in 1985, whilst the density of TUC and non-TUC membership combined was 44 per cent in 1968, 54 per cent in 1979 and 43 per cent in 1985.[14] There can be little doubt that the rise in unemployment has been a key cause of the decline in union membership in the 1980s but the restructuring of the economy which has taken place has to be related to this. The sectors in which unions have been traditionally well organised (large scale industrial and manufacturing sectors) are the ones which have contracted, whilst the sectors which expanded, and in which new jobs were created after 1983 (particularly the private service sector), are traditionally difficult sectors for trade union recruitment and organisation. This is the principal explanation for the fact that the decline in union membership has exceeded the decline in employment since 1979.[15]

The decline in union membership has placed considerable pressure on particular unions, not least in terms of financial implications. The 1980s has been a period of *trade union mergers* of historic proportions, partly but not purely because of financial pressures. Both boilermakers' and textile workers' unions helped to form the GMB, formerly having separate unions of their own. The industrial staff union, APEX, merged also with the GMB.

TASS, the industrial staff union, having distanced itself from the AEU with which it had links, established its own craft section. The former sheetmetal workers' and patternmakers' unions joined it, amongst others. TASS then merged with the major white collar union ASTMS, to form MSF (Manufacturing, Science and Finance). Seafarers' and rail workers' unions merged to form RMT (Rail and Maritime Transport). The civil service unions, SCPS and CSU, merged to form the National Union of Civil and Public Servants. The print workers' unions, NGA and SOGAT, merged to form the Graphical, Paper and Media Union. The EETPU merged with the AEU to form the AEEU (Amalgamated Engineering and Electrical Union). NALGO, NUPE and COHSE merged to form a giant public sector union, UNISON. Furthermore, this is evidently not the end of the list.

However, unions have changed in other ways since 1979, not least in terms of policy. In the 1980s 'new realism' challenged more traditional ideas about the purposes and methods of trade unions, and became the dominant perspective within the trade union movement.

'New realism' might be described as follows. Whether the trade union movement likes it or not, there have been fundamental changes since the Conservatives came to power in 1979, and unions have to change accordingly in terms of new directions and methods if they wish to survive. The days of bringing down Conservative governments through trade union confrontation are gone. Altogether the emphasis needs to be less on the use of industrial action and more on the provision of up-to-date services to members. The way to oppose Conservative legislation is not through breaking the law, and in any case the balloting procedures introduced by the Conservatives are generally popular with trade union members. Confrontation between unions and management is not inevitable, areas of common ground should be sought more frequently and there is scope for some degree of partnership with industry. Nationalised industries were not popular with the public and could not stay as they were. Privatisation may not be the answer, but a future Labour government should not renationalise most of them either. The days of class struggle are essentially a thing of the past and the changes in the structure of the economy are part of a permanent shift from a Fordist to a post-Fordist society. This view was embraced by EETPU policy and the leadership of the AEU, and has been the position of the merged AEEU.

The traditional position of the left in the trade unions is epitomised by the stance of the NUM in the 1980s. It might be described as follows. Whilst a restructuring of the economy is certainly taking place with a dramatic effect on total union membership, the use of industrial action remains relevant. The issues and struggles of the broader labour movement, often expressed through support for other groups of workers on strike, should not be lost sight of, and activists have a responsibility to campaign for and win the arguments about these issues with the membership in spite of the pressures of the media. A central problem is the capitulation of both the TUC and Labour Party leadership to the demands of Conservative governments and the pressure of the media. The Labour Party leadership have made concessions to the Conservatives in a bid to appease the press and win the confidence of big business, an impossible task in a class-ridden society. It is terrified of the prospect of confrontation with big business and the establishment, but confrontation is unavoidable if a future Labour government is to achieve real, permanent benefits for the mass of the population. The trade unions should not give 'blank cheques' to the Labour Party; trade unions should not be subservient to the Labour Party leadership and, whilst a Labour government is worth fighting for, trade union independence must be maintained under a Labour government. Capitalism is founded on an inevitable conflict between labour and capital, and the UK is still a capitalist society.

Of course, the various positions taken by the trade unions on questions of policy and methods do not all neatly fit into either the 'new realist' or 'traditionalist' categories. However, the two categories do have some value in trying to make sense of the fundamental policy debate which has been taking place within the labour movement under the pressures of Conservative government.

The growth of management consultancy

The era of Conservative government since 1979 has certainly been the age of management consultancy. Some companies are established as management consultants in their own right and operate internationally. McKinsey, the company with which Tom Peters has been associated, is such an example. Top consultants at McKinsey were earning in the region of £200,000 as long ago as 1980. Most management consultants earn much less, but it is far from being one of the worst paid jobs.[16] Large accountancy firms also became involved, particularly in the 1980s, in the development of management consultancy services as a spin-off from their main activity. In this case, companies like Price Waterhouse, Coopers and Lybrand, KPMG Peat Marwick and Deloitte Haskins and Sells are amongst the most prominent. In the 1980s, management consultants have been used for an

Reasons why management might use consultants

Generally a management consultant will be brought in for one or more of the following reasons:

- lack of specialised inside know-how and experience;
- to solve a problem faster or speed up decisions;
- to overcome internal managerial conflicts;
- to 'sell' decisions to the workforce and/or lower management;
- to add 'independence' to a joint union-management project;
- as a red herring to draw the trade unions' attention away from other issues;
- to baffle shop stewards with pseudo scientific language and methods, for example 'scientific' job evaluation schemes.[17]

increasingly broad range of activities, not least those associated with new management initiatives: employee involvement methods such as attitude surveys, other human resource management questions, the implementation of total quality management systems, reviews of managerial organisation, strategy and philosophy, just-in-time production, how just-in-time might be integrated with new information technology, and labour flexibility initiatives.

Management consultants adopted a more prominent role in the 1980s, not only through their direct employment by client companies and public sector organisations, but also through their involvement in Department of Trade and Industry activities, and in conjunction with the dissemination of information by and on behalf of the new management 'gurus'.

The DTI has been extremely busy in the 1980s and 1990s producing large quantities of information advocating the merits of just-in-time philosophy, total quality management, planned and integrated new technology systems and employee involvement.[18] It organises promotional 'road-shows' and offers extensive advisory and support services to companies intent on implementing such changes. It has employed management consultants to do much of this work.

Thatcherism has also created a climate in which an increasing number of 'management gurus' have been able to promote their ideas, at a price. Large quantities of books and videos have been sold, offering advice to ailing British and US management. Tom Peters, with his evangelical style of presentation, became one of the most well-known 'gurus' in the UK. His view emphasises the role of ideas, philosophy and the involvement of people in the solution of management problems. It sounds simple enough, and Peters has emphasised the uncomplicated aspect of his ideas.[19] However, in most academic circles in the UK his work has not won much credibility and his books are often perceived as 'pop management'. Other 'gurus' who have specialised in quality assurance issues, and who may have had more influence on changes in UK management practice than Peters, include Philip Crosby, W. Edwards Deming, Joseph Juran and Genichi Taguchi. However, the influence of these management specialists has not been restricted to the UK. In fact, Deming and Juran played a very important role in influencing *Japanese* management thinking as long ago as the 1950s.

Whilst some of these management gurus, management consultants and the promotional activities of the DTI would appear to be an influence on current management thinking in the UK, the extent to which they have actually brought about change in the practice of management in the UK is of course quite a different question (and one which is generally beyond the scope of this book). The aim in the chapters which follow is to explain and discuss the new management methods, to consider their implications for trade unions and to identify possible trade union responses to them in terms of policy and action.

However, before looking at the detail of the new management methods, it is instructive to look at their origins in Japanese and US big business and in the work of management theorists.

Lessons from Japan

The historical origins of the new management initiatives
Post-war management in Japan played a pioneering role with regard to the *development* of new management initiatives and techniques, which has had world-wide implications. However, there is evidence to show that the *origins* of most of these methods were pre-war, and were not all Japanese.

In the 1930s there were some interesting developments at Matsushita, the Japanese consumer electrical appliance company which trades under the National, Panasonic, Technics and Quasar names. Apparently inspired by Henry Ford's low pricing strategy for the Model T car, Matsushita developed such a strategy for its entire product range, recognising the battle for market share as central.[20] However, Matsushita went further. The company linked together the goals of low price and high standards of quality, tied to a particular emphasis on marketing. Two points of importance emerge from this. The first is that these appear to be the seeds of just-in-time methods of production, something normally associated only with post-war Japan. The second point is that Matsushita does not appear to have been alone in considering in the 1930s the possibility of achieving high quality products simultaneously with a low pricing policy. In the USA in 1931, Walter A. Shewhart, for example, argued in a book on statistical process control that cost reductions were a natural consequence of improved quality.[21] Shewhart's book was in fact the culmination of his work on statistical quality (or process) control at Bell Telephone in the 1920s, having introduced what became known as the Shewhart Average and Range Control Chart.[22] One of the possibilities which his approach opened up was a company strategy of high quality linked to low prices.

It is also interesting to note that, in the case of Matsushita, it has traditionally adopted a strategy of following the lead of other companies in the launching of new products, but then manufacturing them for less and marketing them better.[23] At the heart of this 'followership' strategy is an emphasis by Matsushita on production engineering research related to analysis of competitors' products and how to improve on them. This has been a widely-reported strategy of Japanese companies in the post-war period. What is interesting is that Matsushita were doing this as early as the 1920s and 1930s.

The development of employee involvement also illustrates the point that these new management initiatives are not purely a product of post-war Japan. Employee involvement is based on a unitary perspective, that is the idea that the employer, management and workers are one team with common interests. In fact, this was essentially the outlook of the Victorian philanthropists as employers, and can be traced back as far as Robert Owen in the first half of the nineteenth century. The first important example of a profit-sharing scheme in the UK was that of the South Metropolitan Gas Company in 1889.[24] The Involvement and Participation Association (formerly the Industrial Participation Association), an important organisation in the UK with regard to the promotion of employee involvement and participation, was founded as long ago as 1884. There were also significant initiatives by ICI in the UK in the 1920s which were intended to encourage a unitary perspective amongst employees in the company. It is clear, therefore, that the essential principles of employee involvement were being tested out, in one form or another, in countries other than Japan and well before the Second World War.

Quality circles are another example of a method sometimes believed to have originated in Japan. Japanese management did play a decisive role in the application and development of the idea, but the ideas on quality which formed the basis of the early quality circles were first put forward in the USA.[25] In 1946 the Japanese Union of Scientists and Engineers (not a trade union) was established, and in 1949 carried out a survey of Western technology and industrial thinking.[26] This led to an interest in quality control, and visits and lecture tours in Japan were organised for American quality control experts in 1950 (Dr. W. Edwards Deming) and in 1954 (Dr. J.M.Duran). By 1955 leading companies in Japan were beginning to set up total quality control techniques, all of which had been imported from the United States.[27]

There is, therefore, considerable evidence to show that many of the ideas and early principles underlying the new management initiatives and techniques were in existence outside Japan prior to World War Two.

However, this in no way detracts from the point that post-war Japanese management, particularly in the motor and consumer electrical/electronic appliance industries, played a quite decisive role in the application and development of these new management methods. Furthermore, Japanese multinationals in the last twenty-five years have played a decisive role on a world scale in forcing their foreign competitors to adopt similar management methods, and to set in motion a process of diffusion beyond the control of either themselves or their big business competitors. The section which follows looks at the circumstances which led to these spectacular developments in post-war Japanese management.

Class struggle in post-war Japan

The idea that Japan has not experienced class confrontation on a scale known in Europe, and that this is because of a compliant and obedient Japanese workforce more loyal to imperial traditions than to its class, does not seem to be supported by the historical evidence. It would be incorrect to say that Japanese culture contains no traditions of obedience, or that Japanese culture is irrelevant to Japanese industrial relations. But it would also be a distortion of history to omit the significance of class confrontation in the development of post-war Japanese industrial relations. Unfortunately, there is little popular knowledge of this aspect of Japanese history in Europe or the United States, perhaps because perceptions have been swamped until recently by memories of the apalling atrocities committed by Japanese imperialism during World War Two, and perhaps combined with some kind of conspiracy of silence about some of the facts.

On the day of the Japanese surrender, 15 August 1945, thousands of workers in Japan poured onto the streets in mass demonstrations. They were lead by Korean and Chinese workers, the most oppressed sections of sweated labour in Japan, and thousands of Japanese political prisoners who had previously been rotting away in similar conditions to Allied prisoners of war, because of their allegiance to the labour movement. In nine months between August 1945 and May 1946 there were twenty mass demonstrations and uprisings involving a total of 1.5 million workers.[28] This means an average on one demonstration of 75,000 workers every two weeks. Protest on this scale is of revolutionary proportions, and there would appear to be little doubt that it posed a basic challenge to the system of capitalism in Japan. Trade union membership expanded at a phenomenal pace in this period too: membership increased from 381,000 at the end of 1945 to 4.9 million by the end of 1946.[29] In fact, between 1945 and 1948 trade union membership in Japan grew from practically nothing to nearly 50 per cent of the wage-earning population.[30] By 1949 6.6 million workers were in trade unions, with trade union density at a post-war peak of 56 per cent (higher than UK trade union density and much higher than that in the United States).[31] American troops, initially under General McArthur, occupied the country during this period and the situation clearly faced the US government with the very difficult dilemma of how to dismantle the structures of Japanese imperialism and military dictatorship whilst at the same time ensuring the survival of capitalism in that country.

An International Labour Office publication described the situation in the following terms.

> The year 1945 was a particularly bad year for food supply, with the rice crop at only 45 per cent of a normal year's harvest. There were no imports of foods under the military occupation, and many civilian and military repatriates were further crowding the population. Japan was no exception to the rule that a sudden contraction of resource supply would inevitably split a society into opposing interest groups. Psychologically, Japan became a divided country... Many people became devoted followers of Marxism overnight.[32]

The initial response of the American forces occupying the country does *not* appear to have been aimed at crushing these developments, and in fact the indications are that the policy was one of encouraging freedom of assembly, a free press, and trade union and political rights.[33] This policy was motivated evidently by a determination to dismantle the totalitarian system associated with Japanese military and imperial authority, and to ensure that Japan could not re-emerge as a world military power. It had the effect of creating a climate in which the Japanese left flourished. It seems to be a mistake to ignore this brief but decisive period in the development of the Japanese labour movement and to convey the idea that American forces suppressed the left *from the start* of their occupation, as some writers have suggested.[34] However, a point was indeed soon reached at which American policy in Japan became more concerned about the threat of communism than the threat from the Japanese right. The future direction of US foreign policy towards Japan was clarified by 1947, when American forces banned a general strike planned by the Japanese labour movement. By 1949 the political influence of the Soviet Union in Eastern Europe had developed dramatically, culminating in the Berlin crisis. On Japan's doorstep in 1949, the Communist Party led by Mao Zedong was swept to power in mainland China. These events fundamentally influenced American foreign policy. The Cold War had begun and the aim of defeating the Japanese left had now become, not surprisingly, a top priority for both American policy in Japan and Japanese employers themselves.

In 1949 new legislation was introduced in an attempt to restrict trade union activity in Japan. In 1950 the Japanese employers attacked the Marxist and left-wing elements within the trade unions, sacking thousands in the process. The official target for the 'Red Purge' was the communist-led *Sanbetsu* (Congress of Industrial Unions) but, as is commonly the case in such situations, in practice a much broader group of trade union activists became the victims.[35] Three key companies in the electrical appliance and fledgling Japanese car industries became involved in major disputes.

In 1950 Hitachi faced a series of bitter confrontations, which proved that the battle to defeat independent unions was not going to be easy for Japanese employers. At Hitachi the issues were redundancies and a 'red purge'. The union organisers developed some imaginative techniques, including marathon negotiating sessions with management, held in the open air and surrounded by mass gatherings of union members. This was sometimes accompanied by the technique of pinning managers down by the use of sharpened bamboo spears thrust through their clothing, to prevent them running away when negotiations became difficult for them. Whilst the managers were not physically harmed, the spears were shaken from time to time to keep the managers awake during the countless hours of negotiations.[36] Such a scenario was not untypical of Japanese industrial relations in this period.

In 1950 Toyota, a company which built its financial base from the construction of military trucks for the Japanese war machine, involved itself in a ruthless confrontation with the independent trade unions at the company.[37] In 1949 Toyota faced financial difficulties to the extent that it was repeatedly delaying the payment of workers' wages. In response to union protests, management agreed with the union that wages would be paid promptly in future and there would be no job losses, in exchange for a 10 per cent pay cut. In spite of this agreement, delays in the payment of wages continued. The union organised a twenty-four strike in April 1950 as a result. Toyota responded with demands for job losses and for an additional 10 per cent pay cut. Over the next two months a dramatic and bitter confrontation between independent trade unionism and the employer developed. Mass demonstrations and rallies were organised at the workplace and at company housing. Directors and the plant manager were put on trial at mock courts organised by the workers. In spite of all this, the company finally sacked over 2000 employees and inflicted a critical defeat on independent trade unionism at Toyota.[38]

1952 saw the largest number of days of strike action ever recorded in Japanese labour history.[39] In 1953 it was Nissan's turn. What emerged was a classic confrontation between labour and capital, still remembered as such in Japan today. Of four month's duration, the strike was one of the longest in the history of the motor vehicle industry. With the employer imposing a lock-out until workers agreed to new inferior conditions, barricades were built at factory gates and violent confrontation erupted. Nissan was backed by a large bank as well as the US authorities, and this fierce battle against left-wing independent trade unionism at Nissan was driven not least by a determination to inflict a major defeat on the influence of Marxism in the Japanese labour movement. Nissan won the dispute, sacked union activists, destroyed independent trade unionism, and set up a company union based on the principle of company loyalty (motto: 'those who truly love their union love their company'). This dispute was particularly important because it paved the way for a new climate in industry in which company or enterprise unions (*Kigyo-Kumiai*) emerged as key players in Japanese industrial relations.[40]

These industrial confrontations of the early 1950s were followed by two serious setbacks for the Japanese labour movement in 1960: left-wing opposition to a new security treaty with the US government was defeated in spite of mass demonstrations; and the Mitsui Coal Miners' Union suffered defeat in a prolonged strike (known as the Miike strike) against rational-isation and redundancy. In spite of these lost battles, left-wing traditions in Japan were continued, for example through the anti-Vietnam War movement, the mass student demonstrations in the late 1960s, and industrial confrontations of serious proportions following the oil crisis of the early 1970s. Whilst the traditions of the Japanese left, both politically and through independent trade unions, have continued to the present day, it has been forced into opposition in both the political arena and generally in the workplace in key industries in the post-war period.[41]

A point of particular importance is that the defeats for independent trade unionism in the early post-war period in the car and electrical appliance industries laid the foundation for the development of the radical management methods associated with flexibility of labour, employee involvement, total quality management and just-in-time production.

The emergence of new management methods in the motor vehicle industry

In the wake of the defeats for independent trade unionism at Toyota and Nissan, management initiatives to implement widespread functional flexibility of labour, in conjunction with more sophisticated quality control methods and the promotion of company unionism, appear to have been the priority. The establishment of widespread functional flexibility, ie, the abolition of established boundaries between jobs, evidently increased productivity quite dramatically. However, in conjunction with the other initiatives, it opened up the possibilities of a stock reduction policy, and the consequent release of large amounts of capital to finance investment programmes and low pricing policies, as well as the creation of floor space for expansion.

The main companies in the car industry had thus established the prereq-uisites for the successful operation of just-in-time. With the aggressive independent unions of the immediate post-war period, just-in-time would have been impossible because, with its low stock levels, it is vulnerable to industrial action. In other words, the crushing of independent trade unionism at Toyota and Nissan, and the establishment of company unions in full collusion with management, were fundamental to the dramatic growth of the just-in-time system in the car industry. Company unionism was essential for the creation and maintenance of employee 'co-operation' and company loyalty, and the discouragement of class consciousness. It had a key role to play in the development of employee involvement. The establishment of widespread functional flexibility of labour was also an essential prerequisite for the success of just-in-time, since such a system of production is geared up to short runs and the frequent resetting of machinery in order to synchronise production to current customer demand and its frequent fluctuations.

Just-in-time was a revolutionary approach to production and was originally devised and developed by Toyota, which had demonstrated an innovative approach to production and management techniques in the 1950s and 1960s. This was influenced particularly by the insight and production expertise of Taiichi Ohno. In fact, just-in-time was often referred to as the Toyota Manufacturing System.[42] Hastened by the oil crisis of the early 1970s, just-in-time was increasingly adopted by other companies in Japan.

Not surprisingly the interest of companies in the West grew. Many Western companies focused on the *kanban* technique associated with just-in-time, and as a result initially lacked a broader, more accurate vision of what the new approach was about. The *kanban* technique is essentially a simple method of communicating throughout the production line the number of components which need to be produced at any particular time.

Just-in-time is not simply a set of techniques; it is a *philosophy* which integrates a broad range of both new and old techniques.[43]

However, even in advance of the introduction of just-in-time, both total production and productivity in Japan's car industry rose dramatically in the post-war period. A meagre 7,500 vehicles were produced in 1945.[44] Whilst war-time production had been dramatically higher than this, 98 per cent were trucks for military purposes. The 1945 production figure was more in line with the low pre-war levels and related to the late development of the car industry in Japan. By 1951 production levels were ten times those of 1945, and a similar speed of growth was maintained in dramatic fashion throughout the next twenty five years, such that by 1977 the Japanese car industry was manufacturing 8.8 million vehicles. Only the United States exceeded these 1977 production figures. By 1982 Japan was making more vehicles than France and West Germany put together, and approximately four times the number produced in either Italy or England.[45]

Whilst many sets of figures could be used to illustrate the dramatic improvements in productivity, a clear indication is given by the fact that between 1962 and 1973 employee hours required to manufacture one small four-wheeled vehicle fell from 82 to 28 hours.[46] To take another example, in 1968 total employment in the automobile industry was 0.54 million workers with production at the level of 4.2 million vehicles, whilst in 1975 workers employed rose to 0.6 million (11 per cent increase) with production rising to 7.1 million vehicles (69 per cent increase).[47]

An important fact to remember is that the automobile industry has become the largest industry in Japan, and therefore plays a critical role in the Japanese economy.

There is a strong case to suggest that the new management methods adopted by the car industry in Japan, while not the only reasons for its spectacular growth, played a significant part in bringing it about. It has been argued that high investment in new technology was a critical factor in the Japanese car industry's success.[48] This has to be questioned, particularly once just-in-time production was introduced. The new radical management methods were not dependent on high investment in new technology, and just-in-time is a particular illustration of this. The confusion may arise from the fact that the sometimes massive financial savings which can result from the introduction of just-in-time may create the necessary capital to launch an investment programme for the introduction of the latest new technology, which in turn may create further savings.

Japanese exports: motor vehicles, consumer electronics and new management methods

At the same time as the motor vehicle industry grew to take on a dominant position in the Japanese economy, so the latter began to take on an increasingly important and impressive role in the world economy. Japan's export record of manufactured goods, with motor vehicles and consumer electrical and electronic appliances at the forefront, soon presented a serious challenge to the major capitalist economies. Two important developments resulted from this: rival non-Japanese companies had to begin to imitate the methods of Japanese companies in order to compete; and Japanese companies increasingly invested overseas.

Companies in the West which found that they were losing market share to Japanese competitors were soon forced to seek the reasons for such Japanese success if they wished to survive. A process of diffusion then inevitably began to develop in respect of the new management methods developed by the Japanese companies. European and North American companies, primarily in the motor vehicle and consumer electronics industries, were forced to attempt to imitate the new Japanese methods. Very often it was US companies which were hit first, and therefore led the process of imitation.

The early attempts at imitation were often characterised by confusion about exactly what it was that Japanese management were doing which was so different. Early attempts at imitation were also often characterised by failure. Instances were common of companies latching on to one or two particular management techniques, in isolation from the broader strategy and philosophy, and perceiving these as the 'magic key' to Japanese success. In industries other than motor vehicles and consumer electronics, and at companies which are only now turning to the implementation of just-in-time, employee involvement, labour flexibility and total quality management, this type of error is still far from uncommon, at least in the UK. The car industry in the West, however, with the intensity of competition in world markets, had to put these teething problems behind it quickly. In fact, it would certainly appear that the car industry has embraced these methods world-wide, and it acts as a powerful influence in encouraging the adoption of these initiatives and techniques in other sectors of industrialised economies.[49]

However, the international strength of the Japanese motor vehicle and consumer electronics industries inevitably meant increasing Japanese investment overseas, a development which was to have a variety of consequences.

Not surprisingly Japanese motor vehicle manufacturers saw the US market as the real prize to go for. Whilst their early attempts at penetration of the US market were not too successful, their perseverance was to result eventually in a significant presence in the USA. By 1991 there were seven Japanese motor vehicle manufacturers with sites in that country, with a total annual capacity of 1,818,000 vehicles, including light trucks. This compares with three sites in the UK (Nissan at Sunderland, Toyota at Derby and Honda at Swindon), which produced 316,000 vehicles in 1993.[50]

There are several points worth noting with regard to the Japanese multinational presence in the USA. Most Japanese car manufacturers today are keen to 'tailor' their operations in the US to the local environment. This by no means reduces the impact of the management methods; it has quite the reverse effect. Japanese multinationals have made concessions to the local social and cultural environment. However, the fact that such Japanese multinationals have an uncompromising attitude to their own management methods also, ironically, has the effect of linking the Japanese-owned sites more closely to their local economy in the United States. It seems that critics of Japanese multinational companies often mistakenly imagine that uncompromising attitudes to Japanese management methods mean that such companies *prefer* to import more parts and to retain control in Japan.

In fact the opposite is true. Waste elimination, more frequent, faster delivery of smaller quantities of stocks (ie, just-in-time) and co-operation with suppliers over quality and research and development, all demand geographical proximity of component suppliers. Such methods are not feasible if Japanese manufacturing sites in the US were to use suppliers based in Japan.[51] Japanese companies may find it difficult to establish close to 100 per cent local content, but the operation of just-in-time production means that they have no choice but to aim for this as rapidly as possible, and those which lead this race are likely to pose the greatest threat to the US manufacturers.

An important consequence of the development of local supplier networks is that such networks themselves encourage the diffusion of the the radical management methods operated by the Japanese companies. Just-in-time production demands the supply of components and materials in the form of frequent deliveries of small quantities, and with frequent variations in the specifications of components and materials. It demands the best quality at low prices. In other words, Japanese car manufacturers in the US will demand from their local suppliers essentially the same things which they aim to provide for their own customers of finished cars. It is worth noting, however, that the extent to which Japanese manufacturers can exercise influence and control over their suppliers in the US is likely to depend to a considerable extent on factors associated with the scale of production of the Japanese company's site in the US.

A further development which appears to be taking place within Japanese companies with sites in the USA, at least in the car industry, is that decision-making and communications within the managerial structure do appear to have a 'bottom-up' characteristic to them. Management at sites in the US is American and has considerable power to make its own decisions, with Japanese management rarely using its power to veto them. Japanese car manufacturers are likely to shift more design and development to these overseas sites and this process will further strengthen the authority and control of local management. All this cannot be separated from the emphasis placed on employee involvement by Japanese companies. It is effectively employee involvement for local management.

YKK Fasteners was the first Japanese company to establish a site in the UK, as long ago as 1972. Sony set up a site in 1973; and by 1989 it had invested £99 million in the UK, with one of the world's most advanced television manufacturing sites at Bridgend, South Wales.[52] Europe's largest concentration of foreign silicon chip plants was sited in Scotland, with Japanese companies playing a significant role in developing that site. Then of course there are the Japanese car manufacturers in the UK. By 1989 25,000 jobs had been created or safeguarded by Japanese companies investing in the UK.[53] In 1986 there were thirty Japanese projects in the UK; by 1989 there were three times this number.[54] By 1994 there were 200 Japanese manufacturing companies occupying 268 sites in the UK.[55]

The kinds of developments taking place in the UK as a result of Japanese investment, particularly in the car industry, are not dissimilar to those described earlier with regard to the USA. The implications for, and of, local supplier networks as a result of just-in-time production directly relate, for example, to the Nissan site at Sunderland in the UK. The high degree of autonomy for local management of overseas Japanese sites would appear to apply to the UK as well.

There are important differences, however, between the situation in the USA and the UK. Japanese sites in the UK are much fewer in number. They compete in the UK with US multinationals, which have had sites in the UK for very much longer. In fact, the levels of US investment are far higher than the levels of Japanese investment in the UK.[56] This means that US companies in the UK may well have a very significant role in encouraging the growth of the new management methods more commonly associated with the Japanese car and electronics companies.[57] In addition, the Single European Market has been a very important factor in shaping the policy of Japanese multinationals in the UK. That policy has to be considered in the context of Japanese multinational policy towards Europe as a whole, both EU and non-EU.

It is hard to ignore the fact that the UK has long been the country in Europe with the highest levels of both US and Japanese investment, and is way ahead of any other European country in this respect. Because of the extent of American weapons stationed here, the UK has been referred to as a US aircraft-carrier. In terms of economics, as a result of the way in which the UK government has welcomed investment by Japanese car manufacturers, Peugeot's competitive head, Jacques Calvet, has referred to the UK as a 'Japanese aircraft-carrier sitting off the coast of Europe', and as 'Japan's fifth major island', comments which rather upset the European Commission.[58] Part of the importance of Japanese investment in the UK is that it provides a springboard *within the EU* for the European markets, one established prior to 1992 and the imposition of restrictions in the Single European Market for non-EU countries. Fears of 'Fortress Europe' certainly appear to have speeded up Japanese investment in the UK in the run-up to 1992.

The UK has a range of factors which make it more attractive to Japanese investment than other EU countries. An obvious one has been the sympathetic political climate for Japanese multinationals. Not only have Japanese multinationals been directly encouraged to invest in this country by Conservative governments, but also legislation restricts union activity and a climate has been created which has put the trade union movement on the defensive. Low labour costs, compared with most other EU countries, is a factor which has encouraged Japanese investment. The status of English as an international language would appear to be another factor. So too would the fact that Japanese companies have already established a significant presence in the UK, and it is then easier for other Japanese companies to follow, not least components suppliers.[59]

New management initiatives and Japanese industry: lessons for trade unions?

New management initiatives and techniques present a basic challenge to trade unions in the UK in the 1990s. What important lessons might be learnt from the Japanese industrial experience if trade unions are to meet the challenge of new management initiatives more effectively? Several key points come to mind.

The new management initiatives and techniques increasingly experienced in the UK in the 1980s and 1990s are not exclusively Japanese in origin. A greater appreciation of this fact may help to demystify new management techniques, and perhaps discourage misconceptions of them as peculiarly Japanese and rooted in the traditional culture of that country. Union policies and tactics which drift in the direction of anti-Japanese campaigns and encourage stereotypical views of Japanese workers contradict trade union internationalism; it is the latter rather than the former which provides an essential element of an effective, sustainable union strategy towards new management techniques.

The establishment of direct international links between workplace union committees in the UK and workplace independent union committees in Japan (as well as those in the USA where new management initiative programmes are being introduced) is a valuable step for unions to take.[60] Initially, the main practical benefit of such links is the exchange of information on the way in which management are using and developing the new management methods and the possible trade union responses to them at a shopfloor level. This might be followed up by exchange visits of local trade union representatives in linked workplaces. The establishment of direct links would almost certainly reap a range of other mutual benefits to unions in the longer term as well. Unfortunately, much of the international work of UK trade unions is carried out by head office departments and national sub-committees, significantly removed from the daily experiences of the union membership. Direct international links between workplace committees of independent unions in Japan and the UK could be of immense educational benefit. The personal experiences which result from such activity can have profound effects on union members and local activists in terms of encouraging a day-to-day international awareness, which can provide the basis for a deeper union commitment and determination. This may be further developed through the expression of solidarity and practical assistance in the event of union disputes and strikes arising from the implementation of new management initiatives and techniques. The work associated with direct links can be complex and time-consuming, but unions which proceed no further than the exchange of information with independent union workplace committees in Japan stand to benefit considerably in terms of developing a more sophisticated strategy towards new management techniques, which could contribute significantly to undermining their local management's confidence and ability to implement new techniques programmes.

International trade union conferences on new management techniques for particular industrial sectors, of the kind pioneered by the car industry, suggest an important way forward for unions.[61] The international exchange of information and 'networking' between trade union research organisations on the issues also suggests an important way forward. These kinds of initiatives and direct links between workplace union organisations in the UK and Japan (and other countries) are likely to have most effect if they complement each other. The success of such a complementary approach will be partly affected by the extent to which the senior officialdom of the trade union movement are determined to maintain their traditional tight control of international relations between unions. However, the end of the Cold War, and the consequences of this for the reorganisation of international trade union federations, may make this less of an obstacle than it would have been in the past.

Finally, the understanding of new management techniques by trade unionists in the UK, and union strategies in the workplace in response to them, could be enhanced considerably if union research and education departments were to gather and disseminate much more information about the history, current practices, details and points of contact of the independent trade union movement in Japan. Such information could be distributed through union courses, in union newspapers, at conferences and through circulars to branches, district committees and trades union councils. This would not only provide a necessary base of information to promote international initiatives and links of the kind already outlined, but would also convey the important message that new management techniques were established in Japan only after a series of major defeats for the independent, militant trade union movement in that country.

Notes

1   Brian Towers, 'British Industrial Relations: Context, Continuity and Change', in Brian Towers (ed), *A Handbook of Industrial Relations Practice*, Kogan Page and IPM, 1987, p3.
2   *The Guardian*, 15.2.94.
3   Crown copyright. Reproduced with the permission of the Controller of Her Majesty's Stationery Office.
4   The real reasons for Thatcher's departure may well have been associated more with the defeat of the poll tax and Conservative prospects at the 1992 General Election than the issues about Europe.
5   See, for example, the arguments by John MacInnes, *Thatcherism at Work*, Open University Press, 1987.
6   *Ibid.*
7   *Ibid*, p93.
8   *Ibid.*
9   *Privatisation and Cuts – the Government Record*, Labour Research Department, 1990, p25.
10 *Ibid*, p4
11 *Privatisation – Paying the Price*, Labour Research Department, 1987, p23.
12 *Privatisation and Cuts – the Government Record, op cit*, pp30-32.
13 *Ibid*, p32, and IPMS.
14 *TUC Directory, 1994*, TUC Annual Reports; the Certification Officer's Annual Reports; Department of Employment, *Employment Gazette*, February and June 1987; G.S.Bain and R.Price, 'Union Growth: Dimensions, Determinants and Destiny' in G.S.Bain (ed), *Industrial Relations in Britain*, Blackwell, 1983.
15 Brian Towers, 'British Trade Unions: Crisis and Response' in Brian Towers (ed), *op cit*, p23.
16 TGWU and Ruskin College Trade Union Research Unit, *Management Consultants – Friends or Enemies?*, 1983, p14, and the *Institutional Investor*, November 1980.
17 TGWU and Ruskin College Trade Union Research Unit, *op cit*, p16.
18 See, for example, the DTI Enterprise Initiative series of booklets: *The Quality Gurus, Quality Circles, Statistical Process Control, BS 5750/ ISO 9000:1987, Manufacturing Resource Planning, Just in Time* and *Managing into the '90s*. Also the Employment Department Group have published a report advocating the merits of employee involvement: *People and Companies – Employee Involvement in Britain*, HMSO, 1989.
19 For example, Tom Peters and Robert Waterman, *In Search of Excellence* , Harper and Row, 1982, and Tom Peters, *Thriving on Chaos*, Macmillan, 1988
20 Richard Tanner Pascale and Anthony G. Athos, *The Art of Japanese Management*, Penguin,

1986, pp30-31.

21 Walter A. Shewhart, *Economic Control of Manufactured Products*, Macmillan, 1931.

22 Frank Price, 'The management art of making more out of less', *Management Consultancy*, June 1990, p31.

23 Pascale and Athos, *op cit*.

24 Esmond Lindop, 'The turbulent birth of British profit-sharing', *Personnel Management*, January 1989, pp44-47. This refers to an example of the financial form of employee involvement.

25 Incomes Data Services Study 352, *Quality Circles*, p1.

26 Mike George and Hugo Levie, *Japanese Competition and the British Workplace*, Centre for Alternative Industrial and Technological Systems, 1984, pp35-6.

27 *Ibid*.

28 *Ibid*, p30.

29 The Japan Productivity Centre, *Practical Labour Statistics*, 1981 (in Japanese), as quoted in S.Takezawa *et al*, *Improvements in the Quality of Working Life in Three Japanese Industries*, International Labour Organisation, Geneva, 1982, p11.

30 George and Levie, *op cit*.

31 Mike Allen, 'Japan's Unions: a Yen for Unity', *International Labour Reports*, No.27-28, summer 1988, p15.

32 Takezawa et al, 'Improvements in the Quality of Working Life in Three Japanese Industries', 1982, p11. Copyright 1982, International Labour Organisation, Geneva.

33 *Ibid*; also Channel 4 series, *Nippon*, 1990.

34 For example, Mike Allen, *op cit*.

35 *Ibid*.

36 S.Takezawa et al, *op cit*, p12.

37 Satoshi Kamata, *Japan in the Passing Lane*, Unwin Paperbacks, p9.

38 *Ibid*.

39 Takezawa *et al*, *op cit*.

40 Peter Hetherington, 'Perfection in land of rising productivity', *The Guardian*, 5.3.86.

41 Useful sources on independent trade unionism in present-day Japan are Mike George and Hugo Levie, *op cit*, and Mike Allen, *op cit*.

42 It is often suggested that the 'Toyota Manufacturing System' was the original title for just-in-time and that it had its origins in the 1960s. This conflicts with convincing evidence that Toyota have always used the title just-in-time. Also it appears that Toyota originally implemented the system at their new Koromo plant in Japan for the manufacture of military trucks in the late 1930s, as a result of the detailed ideas of Kiichiro. For reasons which are unclear, the system was totally dismantled during the Second World War. After the War, Taiichi Ohno of Toyota revived and developed the system, using kanbans, and later total quality concepts were integrated into the system. Source: Eiji Toyoda, *Toyota – Fifty Years in Motion: an autobiography by the Chairman*, Kodansha International, Tokyo and New York, English edition, 1987, pp56-59.

43 Department of Trade and Industry and Raymond H. Jewitt, *Managing into the '90s: Just-in-Time*, 1989, p2.

44 Takezawa et al, *op cit*, p111.

45 *Ibid*.

46 *Ibid*, p112.

47 Japan's Ministry of Trade and Industry, *Census of manufacturing firms*, and Japan Automobile Manufacturers Association, *Automobile Statistical Yearbook, 1977*, both quoted in Takezawa *et al*, *op cit*, p141.

48 See, for example, Takezawa, *op cit*, p112.

49 On the adoption of these methods in the UK, see N.Oliver and B.Wilkinson, *The Japanization of British Industry*, Blackwell, 1988.

50 Society of Motor Manufacturers and Trades in Andrew Lorenz, 'The British Car is Dead', *Management Today*, August 1994. This excludes IBC, the former Bedford vans plant at Luton, now a joint venture between General Motors (60%) and Isuzu (40%). IBC produced 41,000 vehicles in 1993 (source: *ibid*).

51 'Lean, mean and through your windscreen', *Economist*, 23.2.91, p95.

52 Larry Elliott, '£36m Sony expansion plan', *The Guardian*, 3.2.89.

53 *Ibid.*

54 *Ibid.*

55 Invest in Britain Bureau, Department of Trade and Industry, 1994.

56 Brian Towers, 'British Industrial Relations: Contexts, Continuity and Change' , Towers (ed), *op cit*, p7.

57 *Ibid*, pp7-8. Here attention is drawn to the facts that the total in 1987 of US and Japanese investment in the UK still amounted to under one-half of UK fixed investment in one year, and that Japan's entire European investment remained at only one eigth of its total overseas investment. Towers argues that the impact of these sites on UK industrial relations is more significant than their level of economic activity.

58 Simon Beavis, 'Japan drives up the middle', *The Guardian*, 8.3.91.

59 These conclusions are supported by the comments of Takashi Narusawa of the Japanese City firm, Nomura Securities, in Larry Elliott, *op cit.*

60 This is not to suggest that UK unions would gain from links with any of the various company unions in Japan, which do indeed play an important role in industrial relations there.

61 Transnational Information Exchange/Vauxhall Motors Shop Stewards' Committee Conference, *New Management Techniques – The Development of a Trade Union Counter-Strategy*, Liverpool, Jan-Feb 1992.

Chapter 2

Just-in-time

What is just-in-time?

It has often been stated that just-in-time principles of production are not a new management technique, but a manufacturing *philosophy*. A common, and convincing, line of argument is that the significance of this point has been lost on some sections of British management. The latter, desperate to succeed in the new environments of intensive competition, have often introduced several new manufacturing techniques, copied from the 'Japanese experts', and perceived almost as magic solutions to their problems of flagging profitability. Such sections of management seem to have learnt about the techniques pioneered by certain Japanese companies, but have failed to understand the basic reasons for their introduction in the first place.

This is precisely one of the problems which the Department of Trade and Industry sought to resolve by launching their *Towards Integration* programme in 1987, something which they have followed up in a number of ways since.[1] The DTI material emphasises the principles of the 'new manufacturing philosophy' and the need for companies to audit their current practice, using these principles as yardsticks. The DTI material does not start with detailed explanations of the 101 various techniques of Japanese manufacturing, their benefits and why British companies should adopt them. It also emphasises that increased investment in new technology is not a necessary feature of the new manufacturing philosophy, nor a vital ingredient in the competitive lead of Japanese manufacturing.

An important point is that these apparent misconceptions amongst employers seem to hold sway in some sections of the trade union movement too. The predominant view within the trade union movement is further clouded by the common failure to recognise all the connections between just-in-time production, the various forms of labour flexibility, employee involvement, quality initiatives, teamworking and single union deals, and part of the solution to understanding these connections comes back to an understanding of just-in-time (JIT) philosophy. It is because of this that the DTI's approach to the subject is enlightening for both management and trade unionists.

The basic principles of just-in-time as seen by the DTI

The Department of Trade and Industry's *Towards Integration* programme identified the following basic principles of the new manufacturing philosophy.

1. Make money.
2. Keep the customer happy.
3. Simultaneously
   - increase throughput
   - cut inventory
   - cut costs

   but especially cut inventory.
4. Reduce the time between purchase of materials and payment for finished products by moving the goods more rapidly through the plant. This will cut stock levels, work in progress and quantities of finished goods stored in the workplace.[2]

The DTI's principles 1-3 can be related to profit levels, demand and supply respectively.

Rule 1 emphasises that, if sales are increased whilst reducing both inventory and operating expenses, the result must be to make money.[3] (Inventory means stocks, that is all the money the organisation has tied down in raw materials, components, buffer stocks between machines, work in progress and unsold finished goods.)

Rule 2 – keeping the customer satisfied – relates to better quality of product in terms of its durability, specification and design, and a more competitive price, faster delivery and better standards of after sales service. It is precisely these characteristics which have typified the impact of Japanese motorcycles, cars and electronic goods on British markets over the years. It means that production will be geared up to current customer demand, no more, no less. It means that exactly what is produced is much more closely synchronised to customer demand than it is to the optimum exploitation of investment in machinery, as has traditionally been the case. It means that the aim is to compete in a particular market on the basis of both better quality and a lower price. These things can only be achieved through a more varied and flexible system of production.

Rules 3 and 4 urge us to increase throughput, reduce inventory, reduce costs. Increased throughput, or reduced lead times as it is sometimes called, means that the time it takes under JIT for one particular commodity to be manufactured from start to finish is very much shorter, which allows current customer demand to be met more quickly, and also releases money since the time between the purchase of materials and payment for finished goods is reduced. This means that the level of work in progress is reduced, and in fact inventory/stock levels are driven down throughout the workplace (finished goods, buffer stocks between stages in the production process, components, raw materials). JIT sets 'zero inventory' as its target. This not only releases very considerable amounts of money tied down in 'surplus' stock itself, but also creates extra floor space for productive use or perhaps for sale.

This in turn has a knock-on effect in terms of *quality*: if stock levels are dramatically reduced then the system becomes vulnerable to faulty workmanship since there are not the surplus stocks to make up such losses. Getting the job right first time becomes a more urgent aim. Having established a significant reduction in stock levels, for a JIT system to continue to function there will have to be a dramatic improvement in quality. The logic of the system forces the issue of quality to the top of the agenda, which is precisely the intention. Here lies the link between JIT and quality circles, total quality management initiatives and management interest in British Standard 5750. As the campaigns on quality are organised by management, inspection is needed less, often with production workers stamping their own work, and inspectors' jobs may disappear. The aim of 'zero defects' is added to that of 'zero inventory'. The intention of such slogans is to set targets which in reality can never be attained but always appear relevant. Some critics of the system have argued that it is rather like the thirsty traveller chasing the mirage in the desert.

The logic is that the more you reduce stock levels, the more vulnerable the system becomes to all other kinds of faults or hold-ups, as well as problems of inadequate quality. This creates a situation in which faults and weaknesses in the production process are more noticeable. It forces management to tackle problems as soon as they arise and to find permanent solutions to them, which is not only likely to improve the service to the customer, but also reduces operating costs by making the elimination of all forms of waste a priority. This potential to create a much more effective system of problem-solving and trouble-shooting is a very important ingredient of JIT.

All these characteristics are fundamental to just-in-time production. It is also to these principles that such terms as world class manufacturing (WCM), short cycle manufacturing (SCM), continuous flow production and a 'pull' system of production all refer.

JIT, continuous improvement and 'learning curve economies'

The Japanese concept of *kaizen*, or continuous improvement, is an essential feature of a just-in-time system of production.[4] The notion of 'zero defects' referred to above is a part of it. Since a JIT system means the creation of ever lower stock levels, this sets in motion a never-ending process of problem-solving and continuous improvement which gains a momentum of its own. It triggers off a chain reaction, which management have to respond to or abandon the system. One of the consequences of this is that it is likely to expose inefficient and incompetent management, and demands a solution to this kind of problem too. Whilst JIT is very much a quality-orientated system, this does not mean that the *kaizen* process will not be used to find new ways of speeding up the line when necessary. This approach, when operated by management as intended, destroys complacency and creates a climate conducive to continuous learning and change.

Andrew Sayer's explanation of this is particularly enlightening.[5] He perceives the reduction of buffers as important not only because it releases inactive capital but also because it creates a continual learning process. Just-in-time, or lean production as it is sometimes called, creates a central element of instability in the system, and produces objectives which can never be entirely achieved. As Sayer suggests, the 'learning curve economies' continue long after the learning curves of orthodox firms have flattened out. JIT is very much more than a system focused on minimum stock levels. At the heart of JIT is a complex process of learning-by-doing. Whilst Japanese companies operating JIT were continuously learning and continuously improving their methods of production, Western companies had assumed that they had exhausted all significant possibilities in this respect, and saw relocation to cheap labour countries as the only major area of significant further exploitation. Here lies much of the explanation for Japanese car and consumer electronics firms overtaking their competitors in the West. As Sayer also points out, such Japanese companies may in future combine just-in-time methods with the exploitation of cheap labour overseas to achieve yet greater economies.

JIT and the company's supplier network

The more a just-in-time system is developed, the more it will have a knock-on effect on its suppliers of raw materials and components. It will require more frequent supplies of smaller quantities because of the company's lower stock levels. If the company which introduces JIT is large relative to its suppliers, and its suppliers face keen competitors, then these suppliers may be forced to make certain significant changes or lose the business. As the company develops its JIT system, it is logical for it to strengthen its *local* supplier network, which in turn creates opportunities for further stock reduction.

The Nissan site in Sunderland provides an important lesson here. In its purchase of a greenfield site, Nissan acquired an area of 900 acres, considerably larger than that required for its own factory.[6] Its intention soon became clear: here was the site for a local supplier network on its doorstep, and on its own terms since Nissan was now the landowner. In these circumstances, deliveries of components and raw materials two or three times a day, in smaller quantities than previously thought feasible, become a reality. Whether or not such suppliers become subsidiary companies, they certainly become very dependent on their bigger customer. However, such suppliers usually enter this situation willingly. Suppliers have a lot to gain because they can secure a major contract for their products, and thus secure a significant advantage over their competitors. Nissan gains because it can exert considerable power over its dependent, single source suppliers, and can directly influence product development, pricing and employment relations.[7]

Nissan is the extreme example. Many British firms which introduce JIT do not operate on greenfield sites with single union deals. Nevertheless, any company introducing JIT cannot ignore the problem posed by the need for more frequent supplies of materials and components in smaller quantities. It is difficult to see how this problem can be solved without more emphasis on some variation of a local supplier network. Also, the more such a supplier's business becomes dependent upon a just-in-time customer, the more that supplier will need to adopt a just-in-time system of production itself.

JIT and flexibility

With the need to meet customer demand much more quickly, and the establishment and maintenance of minimal stock levels of finished products, a more flexible approach to production becomes necessary. To ensure that production is more finely tuned to current customer demand, there have to be shorter runs for each model or each version of it , with more frequent change-overs from the production of one model or component to another. The problem which then surfaces from this is the time taken to reset machines, which then has to be done more frequently. Therefore much shorter set up times become essential for the smooth operation of JIT. This is often brought about through the establishment of teams or cells of perhaps six to twelve workers, with considerable elimination of demarcation between jobs within the team. The JIT system, therefore, is likely to pose a significant challenge to trade unions in the workplace because of its consequences in terms of extensive flexibility of working practices. However, other avenues have been explored as well by employers in search of a more flexible approach to production to meet JIT requirements, through the use of new technology.

JIT and new technology

Flexible manufacturing/machining systems

Another way of achieving the desired flexibility of production is through the introduction of new technology in the form of flexible manufacturing/machining systems (FMS), though the relevance of this and the type of system introduced will vary with the industry and the product. Such systems normally operate by means of automatic guided vehicles (AGVs). These are small trolleys on rails, with pallets of mixed components which are machined simultaneously. Machining centres may be equipped, for example, with 80-tool automatic tool changers.[8] Where there is a need to manufacture a small number of large components, the FMS technology may carry out a range of machining tasks on each item simultaneously. However, the investment in the necessary new technology can be enormous, and for most workplaces in the UK it simply does not appear to be cost-effective to see flexible manufacturing systems as an alternative to extensive flexibility of labour, though it may indeed be a useful supplement to it.

MRP II

It is important also to look at the other reasons for the possible use of new technology in conjunction with JIT. JIT is a system which requires precise co-ordination of the production process, highlighting the problem which

The Manchester Employment Research Group on flexibility, cells and new technology

Production must be able to respond quickly to changes in customer demand.

This may result in the development of flexible technology, with short set up times and the ability to switch quickly from one product to another, and a flexible workforce, which can turn their hands to any job required.

This has led to *the development of 'cells'* – a product-orientated layout of manufacturing which places the various machines in the exact sequence required to process a family of parts. Cells are often in straight lines, U-shapes or L-shapes to minimise handling and movement between the processes. These cells are often dominated by a *Flexible Manufacturing System*, which is designed to rebalance at will the production line, rapidly matching output to changes in demand. The FMS involves mixed-model scheduling, multi-skilled operators, standardisation of equipment for quick changeover times and design of the production line to allow workers to do more than one job and to cut down on transportation between lines.[9]

Japanese management know as *muri*. *Muri* refers to an unevenness between different stages in the production process with regard to quantities produced as compared with what is actually needed 'just-in-time'. Independently of JIT, a computerised system known as MRP II (management resource planning), and its fore-runner MRP (materials requirements planning), has been set up in many workplaces for some years now. It serves an important purpose under traditional systems of production. With the emergence of JIT, attempts have been made to tailor MRP II to the new needs of a production process which requires more precise co-ordination.

The *kanban* method

A point which needs to be understood with regard to just-in-time, however, is that the need to synchronise the production process more effectively can be achieved without the use of new technology. The *kanban* method was the original way in which this problem was resolved in the car companies in Japan. A *kanban* may take the form of a small card or marking on the floor, or any other simple sign, which indicates to the previous stage in the production line the type and quantity of raw materials, components or sub-assemblies required at any particular moment. Whilst there are different

The Manchester Employment Research Group's explanation of MRP II

If you are producing 'just-in-time', then each stage of the production process must know in advance what is required of it, when and in what quantity. On top of this, each stage of the production process is reliant on the performance ability of others. The process must be finely synchronized.

Many employers have attempted to co-ordinate the process with the use of information technology and integrating the entire system via computer.

MRP II (management resource planning) addresses operational planning, financial planning and has a capability to answer 'what if' questions. It is made up of a variety of functions, each linked together, such as business planning, sales and operations, master production scheduling, materials requirements planning and capacity requirements planning. Output from these systems should be integrated with financial reports, such as the business plan, purchase commitment reports, shipping budget, inventory projections in dollars, etc.[10]

types of *kanban*, this is the basic principle of the *kanban* method. The communication network starts effectively with a more sophisticated approach to market research which must aim for the very latest information on customer demand. This information is translated into appropriate instructions to be conveyed from the end of the production line upwards through the *kanban* communication network. It is for this reason that just-in-time is known as a 'pull' system of production. Whilst new technology may be used in conjunction with JIT, the *kanban* method is an important illustration of how new technology is not essential to the success of JIT.

Automation and robotics

The reply to the argument that new technology is not essential to the success of JIT might be that Japanese companies are nevertheless leading the way with heavily automated systems and rapidly increasing use of robotics, and this in companies which use the JIT system too. So what is the explanation for this?

It is certainly true that certain Japanese companies are pioneers in the intensive use of new technology, not least robotic systems of manufacturing. It is true that these companies have commonly implemented JIT systems too. A possible explanation is that not only did these companies establish their JIT systems initially without significant use of new technology, but once JIT systems were established, such large cost savings were made that this enabled these companies to operate more competitive pricing policies, improve their profitability and invest in the latest new technology. If this is correct, it raises some interesting questions. It would be most surprising, for example, if such Japanese companies stood still and watched their western competitors learn about and try to imitate their methods in attempts to catch up in increasingly intensive markets. Such Japanese companies are no doubt now attempting to gain economies and a further competitive edge in addition to that gained from their earlier introduction of JIT. [11]

JIT and new technology – a more integrated approach?

There are various forms of new technology commonplace in manufacturing which have yet to be mentioned. An obvious example is computer aided design (CAD), which enables all standard design tasks to be done on computer with better results in less time. Computer aided production management (CAPM) opens up possibilities in respect of accessing and analysing production data, forecasting, and assessing shopfloor capacities. Through computer aided manufacture (CAM) the possibilities of full shopfloor automation become apparent. However, there is a common problem with such new technology; 'islands of automatiom' may develop. From a management stance there is a need to attempt to integrate, to link together the various new technologies introduced into the workplace, and this too can be done through a computerised system. These systems are known as computer integrated manufacture (CIM). The Department of Trade and Industry perceives CIM as a long-term but important objective for companies.[12] It argues that the key to such integration within a reasonable timescale depends on the communication system between these technologies.

However, integration is an issue on more than one level. It is not just a question of integrating the various forms of new technology in a workplace, but also, if JIT is operated, ensuring that those forms of new technology are geared up to the precise requirements and ways of working of the JIT system. In this sense computer integrated manufacture (CIM) has a broader dimension.

The principles of just-in-case production

A clearer understanding of just-in-time can be gained from comparison with what is known as the traditional just-in-case system of production. The just-in-case system has been described as follows.

> Ever since the introduction by Henry Ford of the production line for the model T (between 1908 and 1914), the criteria for manufacturing has been mass production, a system in which the maximum amount has been produced at the cheapest cost per individual item. The argument is that there is a capital outlay, for plant, machinery and labour, regardless of the amount produced, so that the maximum return on capital invested can be achieved by economies of scale. This method supposedly 'pushes' production through the system. The total production then has to be sold. If it cannot, then items left have to be stock-piled, until they can be sold at the asking price, or dumped onto the market at a price sometimes less than the cost of production. This is regarded as typical capitalist production, even in Japan. It is hoped that the demand for goods meets the supply that is possible.[13]

Is JIT a possibility in non-manufacturing work?

JIT is intended as a more cost-effective and profitable system of production. It has been developed particularly in the Japanese motor vehicle and consumer electronics manufacturing industries. Is it possible to apply the basic principles of JIT to non-manufacturing sectors?

Retail companies

Is it not feasible for retail outlets to reduce stocks to the lowest possible levels in order to meet their requirements for the next few days, or week or two, depending on the nature of their products? In fact, it is evident that bigger retailers are already operating along these lines. If JIT is spreading in manufacturing, then bigger retailers are likely to explore the possibilities of demanding more frequent deliveries of particular goods in smaller quantities. Such retailers, which traditionally have retained large stocks in their own warehouses, are likely to aim for major cost savings through the maximum stock reductions feasible. This too can be assisted by the increasingly sophisticated computer systems now being developed to enable more precise and up-to-date stock control in retail companies. There is a significant parallel here between the use of information technology in manufacturing in conjunction with just-in-time, and its use in the retail sector.

Public services

There is also the question of whether it is feasible to apply the JIT philosophy to public services such as the National Health Service, education and other local authority services (housing and social services come to mind). This possibility may be part of the hidden agenda of public sector management, management consultants and government 'think-tanks'.

What is evident in these sectors is that significant campaigns have been under way for some time on quality of service issues. These campaigns are often couched in the jargon of quality assurance and total quality management. Their link to the Citizen's Charter can usually be identified. The application of BS 5750 and the Training and Enterprise Councils' Investors in People standards has occurred in various areas of the public sector. Housing departments and social services have been concerned with reviewing and reorientating such departments to meet 'client need' more effectively within the constraints of tight departmental budgets.

Are these initiatives and campaigns linked to a perception of the service (or the client, student or patient) as a product within a free enterprise culture, and therefore linked to an attempt to apply just-in-time principles to public services? When you consider just how closely related quality improvement is to JIT, the question of whether JIT is part of the agenda of the quality campaigns in the public service sector is a logical line of enquiry.

Another relevant factor is the way in which successive Conservative governments have injected free market style competition into the public services, which has indeed acted as a stimulus to the latter to adopt the philosophy and techniques of private industry in its environment of intensified competition and battles for market share.

Related to this is the widespread use in recent years of management consultants by public services. These are largely the same management consultants which have advised private industry in the UK and the Conservative governments throughout recent years about the management initiatives on quality, JIT, employee involvement and labour flexibility.

An alternative view is that these quality initiatives are nothing to do with JIT, but are the result of severe public spending cuts which have meant that there has had to be a thorough review of ways of working to improve cost-effectiveness. This might be combined with the threat of a fundamental loss of public confidence in public services because of cuts, not least the NHS, and an attempt to counteract this. These arguments cannot easily be dismissed.

The reality could well be a combination of all the explanations mentioned. It does seem unlikely that the new emphasis on quality issues in the public services can be purely explained in terms of JIT, and yet at the same time it seems equally unlikely that established management consultants, with their breadth of experience of private industry and government in respect of the new management initiatives, have not already begun to explore the possibilities of applying JIT philosophy to public services.

Clerical and Administrative Work

In July 1990 two management consultants with Coopers and Lybrand wrote an enlightening article entitled the 'The Office Factory'.[14] This article outlined the principles of JIT and showed how they could be applied to clerical and administrative work and what the implications might be. It has some interesting conclusions which suggest that the application of JIT to office work is perfectly feasible, and that the cost savings, improvement in quality and other knock-on effects could be as dramatic as in manufacturing areas. Their arguments are fairly convincing. Attempts by management in all sorts of sectors (though staff areas in manufacturing are the obvious targets) to reorganise offices along the lines of JIT principles would be a logical development of the application of JIT on the shopfloor. In fact, some manufacturing companies have already taken such initiatives, but with the minimum of fuss and without explicit reference to the underlying JIT philosophy.

In offices information is often the inventory, and therefore the aim of zero inventory means 'zero paper'. As Jolly and Patrick argue, much of the paperwork flowing round the workplace may not be that useful or necessary.[15] How much of it will be consulted again once filed? As on the shopfloor, lower inventory can make problems more visible. Stuffed filing cabinets and overflowing in-trays conceal problems and increase the length of time a job needs to be in the system. Minimum paper in the office would help staff to focus on the organisation's key objectives. This is all apart from the amount of space saved by discarding redundant files.

The concept of set-up times for machinery in manufacturing can be applied to the office too. Repeated telephone calls at inappropriate times can be a major reason for low productivity in the office, since certain tasks require long periods of undisturbed concentration (effectively set-up time) before any significant progress can be made on the task. As with

The JIT perspective and quality circles in the office: Deloitte Haskins and Sells, Birmingham

This well-known management consultancy set up a quality circle in its Birmingham office. It aimed to tackle quality problems at source, embracing the total quality concept of involving all employees in such problem-solving. Issues considered by the quality circle included internal paperwork, the quality of meeting rooms and car parking. One group focused on telephone procedures and came up with some interesting conclusions. Outcomes included a doubling of the number of switchboard operators, the introduction of a simple system to ensure that phones on unoccupied desks were answered more promptly and effectively, and the frequent updating of directories and abbreviated dialling codes. These changes to telephone procedures were perceived as particularly important in providing an impressive service to customers.[16]

the application of JIT to manufacturing, the reduction of set-up times becomes an important objective in the office.

JIT principles emphasise the importance of rapid response to customer demand, and so the identification of causes of delay in the office is a key issue. Typical causes may include concentration on 'production' for its own sake rather than exclusively on what the customer wants, poor quality work (for whatever reason), starting jobs which cannot be finished, inefficient information flows and overcomplicated processes. Total quality initiatives and the elimination of waste inevitably arise as key issues. Linked to this may be attempts to establish quality circles, perhaps learning the lessons from the crude, and often failed efforts of management in manufacturing in the early 1980s (or maybe repeating them, only time will tell).

Why is just-in-time such an issue?

Much can be learnt about just-in-time by looking at the Japanese car industry in the post-war period. Following the defeat of Japan in 1945, that country's economy was devastated. National recovery was dependent on very considerable political, technical and economic assistance from the United States. By the early 1950s Toyota and Nissan were in competition to build up a car industry from practically nothing to one which could establish a niche in foreign markets. Odds were heavily stacked against them, with lack of technical know-how and design ideas way behind those of their western competitors. Three initiatives by the main Japanese car companies made a significant contribution to turning this situation around dramatically.

First, independent trade unionism was directly confronted, defeated and replaced by company unions which co-operated fully with the industry's needs and were organisationally integrated with the company. Second, this situation created an environment conducive to the emergence of a wide range of new management techniques and initiatives, ones which produced major cost savings, placed quality and price at the top of the agenda, and in turn created a very competitive edge to Japanese motor vehicle and consumer electrical and electronic appliance industries. Third, in the 1950s, teams of Japanese car designers and production engineers involved themselves in an intense programme of study of western car industry know-how, with technical assistance and exchange visits organised with US and British company representatives.

In the 1960s the Japanese economy was certainly performing impressively. As the 1970s developed, Japanese big business began to make a serious impact on world markets, particularly in motor cycles, cars and consumer electronics (in fact, Japanese competition destroyed the British motor cycle industry earlier than this). The Japanese government also managed to establish some very significant ties through shrewd diplomacy with Arab states to protect the Japanese economy's vulnerability to oil shortages. The position of western companies in these world markets came under increasing pressure as a result. This occurred, however, at a time when western multinationals were facing competitive problems for other reasons as well.

The oil crisis of the early 1970s sent a shock wave through the western world. The prolonged post-war boom was coming to an end. Many markets were now dominated by great multinational companies with immense productive capability, whilst opportunities in new markets were not as freely available as they were in the earlier post-war period. In a number of sectors big companies turned to the incorporation of new technology in products for markets which had simply not existed before. However, it was the Japanese multinationals which were now in a position in certain industries to adopt another approach as well: through the use of just-in-time in conjunction with widespread flexibility of working practices and the co-operation of company unions, they could sell products which were of better quality of design, better quality of manufacture and were cheaper as well. They did indeed combine this with the latest technology incorporated in sophisticatedly designed products. Japanese multinationals had now commenced a full scale battle for market share, particularly in the motor industry and consumer electronics, and they were winning, with American home markets as well as European under serious threat.

The response of western companies was to seek out the reasons for the Japanese competitive advantage, learn from their success and as far as possible imitate their methods. In the motor industry and consumer electronics, a process had now been set in motion on a world scale which was beyond the control of individual companies, however large.

As we moved into the 1980s, the power of multinationals and the intensification of competition on a world scale, through battles for market share rather than the exploitation of new markets, increased further. In the case of Japanese companies in the 1990s, the on-going intensification of competition is placing pressure on them to change and develop their production techniques in yet more radical directions.

As employers in the UK motor industry and consumer electronics began to adopt the Japanese methods, it was inevitable that many companies in other industries, whether under threat of Japanese competition or not, would investigate and, where appropriate, adopt just-in-time principles linked to labour flexibility packages. Where single union no-strike deals (the Japanese alternative to the establishment of company unions when operating in the UK?) were not feasible, it would at least assist management in their objectives to adopt an employee involvement programme to encourage a workplace culture more appropriate to the new ways of working. A process of diffusion is taking place internationally in respect of these new management principles and methods, with an important emphasis on the USA and the UK.

Essentially, western multinationals believe that Japanese big business has discovered ways of significantly increasing profit margins as a result of major economies in the time taken for the circulation of capital in the process of production, and through impressive increases in the pace and quality of work. Just-in-time philosophy, and the labour flexibility, employee involvement and total quality systems which go with it, appear to be the main ways in which this is done.

Just-in-time: strengths, weaknesses, implications and the trade union response

Stock level and work-in-progress reductions

It is in these areas that clear financial advantages of JIT for employers lie. Instances are given in a British publication of inventories being reduced by as much as two thirds.[17] When JIT is used in conjunction with appropriate computerised systems the results in management terms can be impressive.

Radical reductions of stock levels and work-in-progress brought about by JIT can release very considerable amounts of capital to improve flagging profitability and provide money for new investment programmes. However JIT systems are often introduced into the workplace without significant negotiation with recognised trade unions. Where unions do agree to its introduction, it is usually in the form of some kind of enabling agreement which effectively provides management with a wide range of opportunities to introduce JIT in conjunction with a flexibility of working practices package, relatively unhindered by union restrictions. In the hands of competent management (and indeed this is not always the case), the implementation of JIT can be a financial coup, and, in the absence of effective negotiation by trade unions, one in which union members may have no share.

An important defence of trade union interests within the workplace might be to demand full negotiating rights with regard to JIT, but the prospects of such demands being met by management in the climate of the 1990s do not seem good. So, if workplace unions make full use of existing disputes procedures, might these procedures be adequate for them to respond effectively to the introduction of JIT? Whilst separate procedural agreements to control the introduction of new technology may have a useful role to play here for unions, in light of the link between new technology issues and JIT, there may well be a need for unions to campaign for separate procedural agreements on the introduction of new methods of production in order to defend their interests. Such agreements might include rights to cost savings figures. To negotiate such agreements in the climate of a Conservative government would be difficult, but in a more favourable political climate this could prove to be an important way forward.

A second issue is the possible implications of redeployment and job loss which could occur in both shopfloor and staff areas as a result of major stock level reductions.

The other complex and fundamental question is whether it is feasible, whatever the political climate, for trade unions to oppose the introduction of JIT altogether. This seems unlikely in many industries. However, whilst there is a strong case to suggest an inevitability about the operation of JIT in the mass car and consumer electronics industries, such inevitability throughout all other manufacturing sectors is not yet evident. In some sectors of industry long production runs and relative inflexibility in the organisation of production may be unavoidable because of the type of technology required and the costs involved in its operation.

Just-in-time – 'management by stress'

When well established, JIT becomes a system of production which is much more synchronised or finely tuned than traditional just-in-case systems. The more it is developed, the more sensitive it becomes to faults and weaknesses, not least those of the workforce itself. Those who are not putting 100% into their job become conspicuous, and the finely tuned JIT system will probably mean that this causes problems for their workmates. This is an intended part of the JIT process and is linked to the on-going problem solving approach known as *kaizen*, or continuous improvement. This can create a particularly stressful working environment which has the intention of dramatic improvements in quality and productivity. It has been suggested in the case of productivity, for example, that there are already instances in British and US companies of improvements of over a third as a result of the introduction of JIT.[18] There are good grounds to suspect that it is these highly stressful circumstances in particular which account for the high labour turnover reported at the Nissan site in Sunderland in spite of very high unemployment in that region. Whilst there are obvious advantages to management of such a system, the implications for the workforce of this considerable intensification of the labour process are serious.

- Dependent on the type of wage payment system and the outcome of pay settlements, the workforce may not benefit in their pay packet from the increased workload.
- Job losses may result.
- Labour turnover may increase.
- The consequences in terms of stress-related illnesses may be extensive.

If JIT's introduction into a workplace is negotiated with the union, it is difficult to see how management could make many concessions on these points without disrupting some of the basic advantages for management of introducing JIT in the first place. The 'management by stress' dimension of JIT may be one which unions can only tackle by either

- opposing JIT altogether (which in many circumstances is probably an unrealistic proposition for unions), or
- by linking the introduction of JIT to an additional reduction in working hours *and* by health and safety agreements and provision which give greater recognition by management of the existence of stress-related illnesses caused by industrial working environments.

However difficult these things are for trade unions to achieve, if they fail to respond to the 'management by stress' implications which accompany the introduction of JIT into a workplace, the consequences for trade union influence and credibility in the workplace may be very damaging.

Just-in-time: labour flexibility implications

JIT necessitates increased flexibility of working practices (that is functional flexibility of labour). It reorganises working practices to ensure efficient use of labour in its new system of production which is more closely synchronised to current customer demand, and which means shorter runs and frequent variation of what is produced and in what quantities. JIT may also encourage an increase in the proportion of temporary and part-time labour, and the use of more flexible shift patterns and annualised or averaged hours agreements (known as numerical and temporal flexibility of labour). Another way of looking at this is that, with JIT, management more closely synchronises *the demand for labour* with customer demand. These labour flexibility initiatives which result from JIT, whatever precise form they take, entail several important benefits for management. These will be at the expense of the workplace unions. They include the following.

- A decline in union bargaining power on the shopfloor because of decreased union influence on the supply of labour.
- Increases in productivity not necessarily reflected through increases in workers' wages (depending on the outcome of pay settlements and the type of wage payment system).
- The more efficient use of labour may result in job loss, whether through 'natural wastage', redundancy or both.

On the other hand, it has not been uncommon in recent years for unions to agree to far-ranging labour flexibility packages. There is evidence to suggest that these may have been achieved through wage agreements which were significantly above the rate of inflation.[19] Where such labour flexibility initiatives were needed to assist with the introduction or development of JIT, the savings to management may have been far greater than the unions ever anticipated when negotiating such agreements.

Just-in-time: are British management up to the task?

The other question which has to be asked is whether there is sufficient management competence in many UK workplaces to make JIT production systems work effectively. Doubts about British management's competence in respect of JIT are aroused by several factors.

- In recent years, with the impact of Japanese competition, the response of some sections of management has been to identify the apparent Japanese 'magic solutions' and go for the 'quick fix'. This point has been made by management academics and government alike.[20]
- In the early 1980s quality circles were seen by many companies in such a light. Many of these early quality circles failed. Research suggests that whilst redundancy and company restructuring may have been the single biggest cause of failure (ie, the impact of the recession of the early 1980s), lack of planning, finance, commitment and understanding of the deeper issues by senior management were significant causes.[21]
- Whilst some saw quality circles as the key to Japanese success, others perceived new technology as the 'quick fix'. In fact, the Department of Trade and Industry have recognised this problem, emphasising that high investment in new technology is no substitute for the right philosophy and an integrated approach.[22]

The DTI used the title *Towards Integration: The DTI initiative for competitive manufacturing* for their 1987 campaign to encourage UK industry to adopt the JIT philosophy. Whilst the DTI have published much on the subject of new management initiatives since then, their 1987 publication conveyed a message of continuing relevance. It emphasised the need for integration between design, manufacture and marketing, and stressed the importance of the competence, commitment and knowledge of management. It was particularly critical of any use of new technology to hide management deficiencies.[23]

A primary concern of the DTI was that too many UK companies seem to have thought high investment in new technology was the key to their Japanese competitors' success (along perhaps with one or two techniques like quality circles), and that the sooner they got on with its introduction the better. The DTI were keen to suggest that it was the philosophy which was the key to the situation rather the technology, and it was this new manufacturing philosophy which could integrate design, manufacture and marketing in what could become a more competitive organisation in the market place. It is interesting to observe the similarities here with the approach of the American management consultant, Tom Peters; in fact, there is good reason to believe that Tom Peters' ideas have had quite an influence on the outlook of successive Conservative governments in a number of respects. Peters' repeatedly emphasises the importance of philosophy and ideas, of what he would see as the creative elements, of management in successful companies and organisations, rather than the staid, bureaucratic principles which he associated with many failing companies.[24]

This kind of approach of striving for a more integrated (and less bureaucratic) form of company organisation means not only that a proper understanding of the underlying philosophy of JIT must precede and dominate the introduction of JIT techniques, but also that where new technology is introduced as well it must not be introduced in isolation to JIT. Equally, there are dangers of introducing the latest machinery and computerised systems without having fully thought through how they will fit in to the manufacturing system in the workplace as a whole. This may result in isolated islands of new technology, the investment in which may prove to be far from cost-effective.

Both the example of early quality circles and that of new technology initiatives in the UK illustrate the continuing possibility of a piecemeal approach by UK management in the pursuit of their Japanese competitors' superior management methods. Management may have learnt from the mistakes of the 1980s, but insufficient evidence is yet available to demonstrate that this is the case. Doubts that management have advanced beyond the piecemeal and 'quick-fix' approaches are fuelled by the well documented problem of the low levels of both company and government finance spent on training, relative to European Union partners. There may be inadequate understanding of the concepts at the root of these modern Japanese management techniques because of a lack of will by both government and big business to spend sufficient money on training and education, not only for manual workers and lower staff grades, but also for *middle and senior management.*

Just-in-time is vulnerable to industrial action

It has been explained in a number of different ways how JIT means that production is much more closely synchronised to current customer demand, which means that there is no slack in the system and that faults and weaknesses become conspicuous. Production can be easily disrupted under JIT. In Japan, Toyota and Nissan achieved the defeat of independent trade unionism and its replacement with fully integrated company unions well before they introduced JIT to their factories. They were then in a position to introduce JIT with the confidence that it would not be disrupted by industrial action. This is a particularly important point when related to the attempts to introduce JIT into the UK. *It may mean that JIT is a serious possibility for UK employers only to the extent that trade unions are unwilling, inhibited or prevented from taking industrial action.* The debate then about the prospects for the effective implementation and diffusion of just-in-time in the UK cannot be separated from the following factors.

- The impact of high unemployment on industrial action
- The reduction in union membership and organisation as a result of the restructuring of the UK economy since 1979
- The impact on industrial action of the dramatic changes in the law since 1979
- The growth of 'new realism' in union policy since the mid-1980s
- The growth of single union no-strike agreements
- The considerable interest amongst UK employers since the early 1980s in employee involvement programmes, which are intended to encourage a new workplace culture, and play their part in discouraging industrial action.

There are, therefore, a substantial range of arguments to support the unoriginal but important conclusion that perhaps the most significant means at the disposal of the trade union movement to affect the introduction of just-in-time production is to defend the unions' right to strike from the wide range of attacks it has faced, some obvious, some more subtle, since 1979.

The 1988 strike at Ford's, Dagenham, was the first well-known example in the UK of unions exploiting this weakness of just-in-time. Within days of the commencement of the strike Ford experienced a knock-on effect, with enforced lay-offs at the Belgian site. The British car companies of the 1960s, with their just-in-case methods and large stocks, could withstand strikes for weeks on end, and in some cases it is believed that strikes were provoked deliberately by management to reduce excessive stocks and save on wage costs at the same time. Whilst Ford's unions did herald the 1988 strike as a victory, it is feasible that the unions could have exploited the vulnerability of JIT considerably more than they did. It is also ironic that the flexibility of working practices was a central issue of the dispute, since the importance of such flexibility was directly related to the introduction of JIT in the first place.

Effective defence by trade unions of the right to strike would have two likely implications for those employers contemplating the implementation of JIT production.

1. Some employers would be more likely to delay or avoid the introduction of JIT wherever they can possibly get away with this in their particular market or industrial sector.

2. Other employers, in spite of this, may implement JIT because of a necessity to compensate for the competitive advantage which may have been gained by other companies in the same market through the adoption of JIT production. On the basis of an assessment of the relative risks, such companies may conclude that the organisation of industrial action at their sites is still less likely than being forced out of business by their competitors because of failure to adopt JIT and its associated practices.

On the other hand, the more that unions in the UK fail to defend effectively their right to take industrial action, whether this is at national or workplace level, and in whatever forms the attacks on this right may come, the more that employers will be encouraged to adopt and develop just-in-time production with all its implications for workers and trade unions.

Notes

1 Department of Trade and Industry, *Towards Integration: the DTI Initiative for Competitive Manufacturing*, 1987.
2 *Ibid*, p9.
3 *Ibid.*
4 *Kaizen* derives from two Japanese characters: *kai* – to modify, and *zen* – goodness. The deeper philosophical meaning of *kaizen* is not easily conveyed in the English translation.
5 Andrew Sayer, 'New developments in manufacturing: the just-in-time system', *Capital and Class*, 1986, No30, p53.
6 Tyne and Wear County Association of Trades Councils, *Nissan and Single Trade Union Agreements*, p11; Philip Garrahan, *An Invitation to Sunderland: Corporate Power and the Local*

Economy, a paper presented to the Conference on the Japanisation of British Industry, UWIST, Cardiff, 17-18.9.87.

7   Tyne and Wear County Association of Trades Councils, *op cit*, p10; Philip Garrahan, *Capital and Class*, winter 1986, No27.

8   Two detailed examples of how these systems can work (Leyland Bus and Yamazaki's Mazak machine tool factory at Worcester) are explained in 'Dissimilar Products, Similar Philosophy', *Machinery and Production Engineering*, 16.9.87, pp38-44.

9   Lynne Humphrey, Manchester Employment Research Group, *Just-in-time and Computer Integrated Manufacturing*, a briefing paper for Tameside Metropolitan Borough Council's Employers' New Offensive Conference, 17.11.90.

10   *Ibid*

11   In this context, a third advantage may be exploited by Japanese companies on top of the two already mentioned here. Whilst Japanese companies were setting up JIT systems, western companies turned more to relocation to countries where cheap labour was available as a solution to problems of competitiveness. Japanese multinationals are yet to fully exploit these opportunities for cost saving and competitive advantage. This point is made by Andrew Sayer, *op cit*

12   Department of Trade and Industry, *op cit*, p13.

13   John Pemberton, *New Technology*, Briefing Paper No1 for the Employers' New Offensive Conference, organised by the Manchester Employment Research Group for the Manchester, Bolton and Preston District Committees of the Confederation of Shipbuilding and Engineering Unions, 17.2.90, Salford. For an excellent brief account of the introduction of conveyor assembly line production by Ford, see Harry Braverman, *Labor and Monopoly Capital*, Monthly Review Press, 1974, pp146-50.

14   Andy Jolly and Alan Patrick, 'The Office Factory', *Management Today*, July 1990.

15   *Ibid*

16   *Ibid*

17   C.A.Voss (ed), *Just in Time Manufacture*, IFS Publications, 1987.

18   *Ibid*

19   John McIlroy, *Trade Unions in Britain Today*, Manchester University Press, 1988, pp207-09.

20   See, for example, R. Collard and B. Dale, 'Quality Circles – why they break down and why they hold up', *Personnel Management*, February 1985, and Department of Trade and Industry, *op cit*

21   Dale and Hayward's survey, University of Manchester Institute of Science and Technology, 1984, results summarised in *Incomes Data Services*, IDS Study No352, p11.

22   Department of Trade and Industry, *op cit*

23   Department of Trade and Industry, *Towards Integration*, 1987, p3.

24   Thomas J. Peters and Robert H. Waterman, *In Search of Excellence*, Harper and Row, 1982; also Tom Peters, *Thriving on Chaos*, Macmillan, 1988.

Chapter 3

Labour flexibility

'Flexibility': what does it mean?

Flexibility is a confusing and ambiguous term, not least when it is applied to industrial relations. When employees are urged to operate more flexibly to assist their company or organisation in a period of change or greater competition, to refuse to do so has a certain connotation. To be portrayed as inflexible suggests that you have an indefensibly negative approach to your work. The term flexibility is very much a product of the 1980s and 90s, and with good reason it can be seen as an ideologically loaded concept. Flexible employees are versatile, quick-thinking and ready for anything; inflexible employees are hide-bound, bureaucratic and resistant to change.[1] It has certainly been a difficult concept to challenge, not least for the political opponents of Thatcherism. Another difficulty with the term is its common usage without qualification; simply to refer to the need for greater flexibility in industrial relations or greater flexibility in the workplace does not mean a great deal.

The focus of attention in this chapter is *the flexibility of labour*. Flexibility of pay is another issue, and some consideration of this is given in the chapter on employee involvement (see the references to financial involvement).

Functional flexibility
The term flexibility can refer to the breaking down of demarcation between jobs, and the ease with which workers can be transferred between different tasks. This may be between certain skilled jobs and other skilled jobs, between certain skilled and certain semi-skilled jobs, or may involve unskilled workers. This type of flexibility can occur in any workplace, can relate to manual or white-collar and professional workers, and is a major

issue in sectors as diverse as engineering and further education. It may be brought about because of changes in work tasks due to the introduction of new technology, because of an employer's need for cost savings, or because it is an important component in a broader new management initiatives programme, or it may be introduced by management independently of such factors. This kind of flexibility is sometimes referred to as functional flexibility, since it is concerned with the tasks or functions of particular jobs. This is quite a useful concept, and will be used as a basis for much of the explanation and discussion in this chapter.

Numerical flexibility

Flexibility of labour, however, may come in other forms. Management may employ significant numbers of temporary and part-time workers. Management may sub-contract work which was previously done in-house. This is a means of trying to establish a more flexible and responsive supply of labour; it is an attempt to synchronise more closely the quantitative supply of labour to the immediate requirements of the firm. This is sometimes referred to as numerical flexibility, a useful concept for clarifying developments at the workplace.

Temporal flexibility

Some industrial relations specialists have identified a third category of labour flexibility, concerned with the flexibility of labour time.[2] Known as temporal flexibility, this refers to changes in shift patterns, structure of the working day, flexitime systems, length of the working week and averaged and annualised hours agreements. The temporal flexibility concept is also useful, and alongside functional and numerical flexibility of labour it is adopted throughout this book. In recent years there has been a considerable growth of interest by UK employers in temporal flexibility in terms of the introduction of more complex shift patterns and arrangements for averaging hours calculated on an annual basis.

The flexible firm

1985 was an important year for industrial relations and new management initiatives in the UK. After 12 months of bitter strike action, the miners were forced back to work. In the same year, Nissan secured an agreement of major importance with the engineering union, the AUEW (now the AEEU). This was the the single union no-strike deal for the major greenfield site

> **How a trade union officer explained the meaning of flexibility to an Institute of Personnel Management conference**
>
> In the sporting arena I have mainly observed flexibility at the Arsenal Football Club. Virtually all the team are highly flexible, running all over the pitch, passing the ball, mostly sideways, and scoring very few goals. What is really missing, are the goal-scoring specialists who could change a hard-working modest outfit into a winning team. The same could be said of British industry.[3]

at Washington, near Sunderland.

However, it was also the year in which two other less well known, but enlightening events took place. In October 1985, the Institute of Personnel Management annual conference had the issues of flexibility and employee involvement as key themes. The speech of Dr James McFarlane, the then director-general of the Engineering Employers' Federation, was particularly significant for several reasons.[4] First, it emphasised the theme of labour flexibility as an essential management campaign for the 1980s, the issue which employers in engineering were to link to the 35 hour week negotiations with the engineering unions. Second, McFarlane put the case for single union no-strike deals as the ideal foundation for a full labour flexibility package, employee involvement and much else beside. Third, he suggested employers might adopt a multi-tier labour force. He put the case for companies to sub-contract certain services (catering, for example) and increase the proportion of temporary contracts for a range of jobs. He argued for companies to create an inner core of skilled workers on relatively good pay and conditions, and with greater job security, but operating extensive functional flexibility of labour.

It is enlightening to note that it was also in 1985, in the context of these debates and events, that John Atkinson's research was published which explained his now well-known concept of the flexible firm.[5] The similarity between the views of Atkinson and McFarlane is obvious. These views have clearly influenced the thinking of many employers in engineering, not least British Aerospace, the dominant employer in the Engineering Employers' Federation. However, the flexible firm concept has gained a much wider influence on employers and management in other industrial and non-industrial sectors. In spite of this, Atkinson's flexible firm model has faced considerable criticism for several reasons. Before assessing these criticisms, however, the model itself needs to be explained.

Atkinson's model of the flexible firm [6]

Atkinson's concept of flexibility does not refer exclusively to labour flexibility, whilst it excludes the separate category of temporal labour flexibility. He identifies three categories of flexibility: functional, numerical and financial. Atkinson sees financial flexibility as the flexibility of wage payment structures to encourage and support the operation of numerical and functional flexibility of labour, and it is the latter two forms of flexibility upon which his flexible firm model is built. Atkinson's argument was that companies are moving towards a more flexible structure in terms of the employment and utilisation of labour, and his model was an attempt to describe that structure. He identified a dual labour market for such a firm along the following lines.

The firm would have a *peripheral* workforce, based on *numerical flexibility*, and focused on the external labour market. This may be made up of as many as three groups or bands. At the outer edge is sub-contracted work, carried out possibly by specialist self-employed workers on short-term contracts or by bigger commercial sub-contractors, and work carried out by agencies specialising in the provision of temporary staff. The second group dominated by numerical flexibility are those employed directly by the firm, but with little job security. This is labour predominantly in the form of temporary and/or part-time workers. Such workers have little legal protection and are easily hired and fired. The company may target such recruitment by taking advantage of high turnover rates, and secure a significant proportion of such numerical flexibility through natural wastage and a policy of not filling vacant permanent full-time jobs. A third group in this peripheral labour market for the firm might be trainees working within the firm who are subsidised through government schemes. This peripheral workforce is characterised as a whole by relatively poor pay and conditions.

The flexible firm's peripheral labour market, based on numerical flexibility, is contrasted by its internal labour market which is based on *a functionally flexible core group*. This core workforce experiences relatively good pay, good conditions and job security essentially in return for widespread functional flexibility of labour. The retention and development of skills and competencies specific to the core workforce, ones which cannot easily be bought in, is an important objective of the flexible firm. [8] Atkinson points out that they are not necessarily the most highly skilled

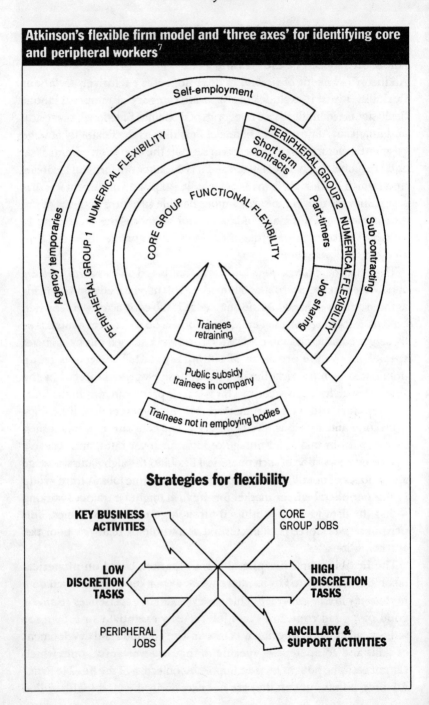

Atkinson's flexible firm model and 'three axes' for identifying core and peripheral workers[7]

Self-employment

PERIPHERAL GROUP 2 NUMERICAL FLEXIBILITY

Short term contracts

Part-timers

Sub contracting

Job sharing

CORE GROUP FUNCTIONAL FLEXIBILITY

Agency temporaries

PERIPHERAL GROUP 1 NUMERICAL FLEXIBILITY

Trainees retraining

Public subsidy trainees in company

Trainees not in employing bodies

Strategies for flexibility

KEY BUSINESS ACTIVITIES

CORE GROUP JOBS

LOW DISCRETION TASKS

HIGH DISCRETION TASKS

PERIPHERAL JOBS

ANCILLARY & SUPPORT ACTIVITIES

workers, but rather those who have the skills most relevant to the company's main activities. For this core group, training is likely to be emphasised to assist the functional labour flexibility required.

Three sets of management motives are identified for the introduction of various forms of labour flexibility. The 'somebody else's problem' approach refers to passing on the flexibility requirement by increasing the proportion of work put out to contract, which, it is argued, will only work where the contractor has specialist skills or experience, or has 'fewer industrial relations restraints' (Atkinson's euphemism, it would appear, for non-union labour). Reducing labour costs is another motive: greater functional flexibility may enable staffing level reductions; greater numerical flexibility may mean big savings on non-wage costs (sick pay, holiday pay, pension contributions, redundancy pay, etc.), and also savings because of easier adjustment of the size of the workforce to changes in demand. The third motive, the 'buffer effect', is an important part of Atkinson's argument. He suggests that very real job security can be achieved for core workers since peripheral workers should be the focus of the firm's numerical flexibility policies. It is the insulation of core workers from numerical flexibility and its associated job insecurity which underpins the functional flexibility of the core group.[9]

If employers' motives for the introduction of numerical flexibility are simply concerned with cheap labour and short-term cost savings, rather than with a broader, long-term flexible firm strategy, then the core workers may perceive a serious threat to *their* job security. In the absence of job security, core workers may well resist management initiatives on functional flexibility.

When Atkinson's study was published in 1985, he expressed the view that relatively few companies in the UK had explicitly and comprehensively reorganised their workforce on the basis of his flexible firm model. He thought most were drifting in this direction, but pragmatism and opportunism dominated management staffing policies.

Criticisms of Atkinson's flexible firm model
It has to be said that there have been many criticisms of Atkinson's model.

i. There have been criticisms because of confusion over what the flexible firm model is intended to be. Is it intended to be a description of how an increasing number of firms are operating in the UK? Is it intended to predict how many firms will operate in the future? Is it a description of how firms ought to operate? It has been argued that Atkinson's work does not make this clear.[10]

ii. Whilst it is intended as a model of the *firm*, it has been criticised because it may actually be a better description of the labour market in the UK as a whole. Advocates of the model may have discriminated insufficiently between the two sets of issues.[11] There is evidence to suggest that this broader labour market has become more segmented since the economic developments of the late 1970s/early 1980s. This is related to the contrasting expansion of service, retail and other non-manufacturing sectors and the decline of manufacturing sectors of the UK economy, with the former emphasising numerical flexibility through its extensive use of part-time and temporary labour. The point is that many non-manufacturing sectors have traditionally operated a greater degree of such numerical flexibility, and with the considerable growth of these sectors in the 1980s, the importance of numerical flexibility in the economy has grown proportionately. The extent to which a core has emerged in manufacturing is questionable, however, in light of the recession of the early 1980s and the even deeper one of the 1990s, with the consequence of considerable job insecurity. Incomes Data Services have argued that possibly an amended version of the model might be useful for discussion of employment patterns across the economy as a whole.[12]

iii. Anne Pollert has argued that there has been no dramatic shift of emphasis by management to labour flexibility, even though the issue was alive in the 1960s and 1970s, being a central element of the productivity bargaining of the time.[13]

iv. Neither was there evidence, according to Pollert, to show that a *deliberate managerial strategy* of large companies along the lines of the flexible firm model was emerging. Whilst she put forward these arguments in 1987, there are good grounds to believe that they are still valid in the 1990s. She argued that whilst there may be plenty of evidence of the growth of numerically flexible labour, there is no evidence in the private sector to show that this is a *deliberate strategy* to create a peripheral workforce related to a core. In support of the view that there is a lack of a 'flexible firm' managerial strategy, the TUC have argued that many companies which have introduced flexibility packages, have ended up with skills shortages, problems in co-ordinating the use of contractors, inadequate training provision and similar problems.[14]

Much of the expansion of insecure and irregular work can be explained by sectoral shifts in the structure of employment, by cost-cutting measures, and by rationalisation; other changes reflect a host of managerial practices and not simply a strategy of flexibility.[15]

v. The division of the workforce into a core and periphery appears to be simplistic. As suggested earlier in a slightly different context, core workers may effectively have no more job security than peripheral workers. In addition, the identification of core tasks may not be as straight-forward as the flexible firm model implies. The flexible firm model places sub-contracting on the periphery, for example, but is this necessarily appropriate? Sub-contractors often perform critical work, such as maintenance, which may be more accurately described as a core function. As a result many employers operate a more permanent relationship with sub-contractors and exercise close control over their activities.[16]

vi. There are also serious doubts about the extent of any trend towards widespread functional flexibility within the core workforce of firms, however the core might be defined. Whilst certain kinds of changes in working practices may be common, this is not necessarily an indication of the extent of functional flexibility. Dr Michael Cross' research, for example, suggests the extent of functional flexibility is generally limited, with any extensive integration of skills rare outside the environment of greenfield sites.[17]

vii. The flexible firm model fails to recognise the significance to the debate of lack of investment in training. To establish an extensive programme of functional flexibility in a firm, considerable investment in training will be required. However, the absence of sufficient levels of investment in training by either employers or central government is perceived by many as a key weakness of the UK economy. In addition, the flexible firm model has been criticised on the grounds that to operate it requires a fully integrated approach by management to training, re-training and recruitment, something which many firms lack.[18]

viii. Current patterns in pay bargaining are complex and do not fit simply into the flexible firm model.[19]

ix. The model fails to take into account the effects of collective bargaining, and the restraints placed on the actions of many employers at many workplaces as a result, in spite of serious reductions in union bargaining power in recent years.[20]

x. If the model is perceived as something which companies can and should strive for, then it ignores the possible effects of an alternative political environment to that created by Conservative governments. Such an alternative political environment might create other options and ways forward for employers in respect of changes in employment patterns.[21]

So what are the practical implications of all this for labour flexibility issues in the workplace? It is hard to ignore the extensive criticisms of Atkinson's flexible firm model, and the key conclusions seem to be these.

Very few firms, if any, are on the brink of a major break-through of making the flexible firm model a reality. The exceptions may be greenfield single union sites, but even here there have to be doubts as to whether employment patterns conform to the flexible firm model as outlined. Moreover, whether or not there are defeats for trade unions at the workplace, there may still be intrinsic contradictions and difficulties for employers in realising the flexible firm model at all.

Increases in both numerical and functional flexibility of labour alone do not indicate that a particular employer has adopted the flexible firm model. These initiatives are more likely to be based on short-term, cost-cutting exercises, often in the absence of a real managerial strategy. To confuse the two may be to give management more credit for such initiatives than is due. To assume that the employer has already adopted the flexible firm model as a strategy may lead to inaccurate predictions of future management initiatives on flexibility. In itself, such an assumption by workplace unions could encourage a fatalism, demoralisation and sense of defeat amongst their members. The reality is much more likely to be that management, whilst making serious efforts to increase labour flexibility in the workplace, is not really in command of the issue in the way in which the flexible firm model suggests. At the same time, this is not to underestimate the challenges for unions posed by management initiatives on labour flexibility.

Labour flexibility: the 'blockbuster agreements'

In many respects the flexible firm debate may have been wishful thinking on the part of government, some employers and sections of the media. It may have been brought about, to a significant extent, by the 'blockbuster agreements' on labour flexibility which received considerable attention in the mid-1980s. These agreements remain proportionately few in number, but have been given a high public profile. Some were introduced at greenfield sites, the most well-known example being Nissan. Others were introduced at established sites in engineering and manufacturing sectors. Most blockbuster deals at such established sites were introduced in the early and mid-1980s. In the later part of the 1980s, a small number of blockbuster deals were still being negotiated, primarily, but not only, in the chemicals industry. In fact, throughout the decade these kinds of deals have been common in the chemical industry, with typical examples at Shell (Carrington), Shell (Stanlow), Mobil (Coryton, south-east Essex) and Tioxide (Grimsby).

Nissan

The functional labour flexibility elements of the 1985 Nissan agreement with the Amalgamated Union of Engineering Workers (as it was then known) were founded on the fact that only two shopfloor grades existed throughout the plant. These were 'manual worker-manufacturer operators' (or 'manufacturers') and 'technicians'. Manufacturers were not only responsible for assembly work, but also materials handling, cleaning up, first line maintenance and quality assurance. Technicians were intended to become multi-skilled craftsmen eventually.[22] However, to assume that the agreement avoids flexibility between these two grades is mistaken, since it states that the Paragraphs 1 and 11 flexibility principles of the agreement over-ride occupational classifications.[23] Teamworking is central to the way in which functional flexibility is operated at Nissan. The agreement also makes provision for extensive numerical flexibility in the form of temporary and part-time labour (in fact, Nissan established the practice of an initial three month probationary period for all employees). It also introduced temporal labour flexibility through its shift arrangements and financial flexibility in the wage structure.

IBC at Luton (formerly Bedford Vans)

The agreement in question at this factory was effective from August 1987, and was put forward as a survival plan for what was formerly General Motors' Bedford Van and Press plant. The agreement was the basis for a joint venture between General Motors and the Japanese Isuzu Motors. Unions recognised are AEEU, TGWU and MSF. There were nearly 400 redundancies, mostly voluntary, leaving a workforce of 1350 by 1988.[24] The agreement is interesting not only for the flexibility clauses themselves, but also for the fact that it contains a clause explicitly agreeing to the progressive introduction of just-in-time production, and also particularly detailed and sophisticated sections on the team concept and teamworking. Not surprisingly, teamworking at IBC was intended to be the main means by which functional flexibility of labour would be introduced. In respect of labour flexibility, this agreement has to be described as a blockbuster deal.

Labour flexibility: extracts from the Nissan agreement

1. General Principles...

b. i. to establish an enterprise committed to the highest levels of quality, productivity and competitiveness using modern technology and working practices and to make such changes to this technology and working practices as will maintain this position...
iv. to respond flexibly and quickly to changes in demand for the Company's products...

8. Appointment

a. Confirmation of an established appointment with the Company will be subject to satisfactory completion of a probationary period. Normally this will be for three months but when overseas training is incorporated into the first three months of employment the period will be extended accordingly.
b. The Company may at its discretion extend the probationary period. During the probationary period employment may be terminated by the Company or the employee giving one week's notice to the other.
c. The Company may at its discretion hire temporary or part-time employees to cope with seasonal or short-term fluctuations in work levels...

11. Working Practices

a. To ensure the fullest use of facilities and manpower there will be complete flexibility and mobility of employees.
b. It is agreed that changes in technology, processes and practices will be introduced and that such changes will affect both productivity and manning levels.
c. To ensure such flexibility and change employees will undertake and/or undertake training for, all work as required by the Company. All employees will train other employees as required.
d. Manning levels will be determined by the Company using appropriate industrial engineering and manpower planning techniques...[25]

Like the Nissan agreement, it provides for full flexibility and mobility of employees, regardless of occupational classification, of which there are nine at IBC.

Labour flexibility: more recent trends and evidence

Whilst the arguments and evidence of Anne Pollert and others create justifiable scepticism of the flexible firm model (either as a statement of trends or of how things could be), evidence produced by the Incomes Data Services for 1986 to 1990 suggest that 'blockbuster agreements' on functional flexibility were also untypical of workplace trends of this period.[26]

It has already been explained that, in spite of the extensive doubts about its validity, the debate about the flexible firm model still needs to be considered and understood since, however misplaced, it still retains an influence over both management and trade union thinking, serving to suggest that the developments in labour flexibility at the workplace are much more advanced and sophisticated than they probably are in reality.

Similarly in the case of blockbuster deals, it would be a mistake to conclude that because the evidence suggests that they are untypical of the general trend in respect of workplace labour flexibility, they can be largely ignored. In the wake of the 1984-85 Miners' Strike the Conservative government made it clear that they saw Nissan as the flagship in the UK for the new-style industrial relations. In the same vein, the blockbuster deals have also set an example for other employers to emulate in pursuit of the new industrial relations, which, regardless of the numerical significance of such agreements, poses a serious challenge to trade unions.

In respect of the trends in labour flexibility in the workplace, Incomes Data Services' research provides some important evidence for the 1986 to 1990 period which supports the view that functional flexibility of labour in union workplaces has not progressed as far as superficial impressions would suggest.[27]

i. Incomes Data Services (IDS) concluded that for most companies flexible working is based on slow change over a number of years. Initially enabling clauses or agreements are often used to establish the principle of flexible working, and are built on and enlarged later.[28] More precisely, in their review of flexibility over the period 1986-90, IDS believe that overall the process of change was more gradual than prior to 1986.[29] The wide diversity of labour flexibility arrangements is apparent from its review of this period, and it warns against generalisation. There is further rejection

---

Labour flexibility: extracts from the 1987 agreement at IBC, Luton (formerly Bedford Vans)

Working Practices...

ii. to ensure the fullest use of facilities and manpower there will be full flexibility and mobility of employees...

v. to avoid short term fluctuations in the core employee levels, the company may at its discretion recruit temporary or part-time employees or contract out work...

Flexibility and Mobility

The management accepts that full flexibility and mobility will be reasonably applied, that is to say:

i. employees must be properly trained to carry out all work to the required standards, e.g. quality and safety;

ii. employees will not be required to carry out work which is beyond their medically established ability; and

iii. to the fullest extent possible employees will be deployed in such a way that maximum use can be made of their skills and talents.

For their part, all employees are required to accept that:

i. they will carry out any work within their capability, being re-assigned as necessary irrespective of their job responsibilities and/or classification; and

ii. as required they will train other employees or undertake training themselves. ▶

---

of the flexible firm model, which IDS perceives as very much a paper concept; and it notes that where blockbuster deals had occurred (at least in 1988), they had often been preceded by employee involvement and related initiatives aimed at changing attitudes.[30]

ii. Enabling agreements on functional flexibility appear to take more than one form. Some commit unions in principle to fairly specific changes, but allow for much local discussion. Others are more about laying the 'cultural foundation' for future change in respect of flexibility, by securing agreement with unions on general principles and objectives. Securing the real change desired by management may be over quite some years. Furthermore, the IDS research found that with a significant proportion of the agreements studied in 1990, management had been prepared to hold negotiations over periods of 18 months or more, indicating possibly an

◄ Full flexibility and mobility will be one of the basic requirements set
out in each occupational classification. Employees operating to this
principle and whose job performance meets requirements will have their
salary protected.

Occupational Classifications...
The company intend in due course to seek discussions with the Company
Joint Council on the principles of providing for individual variations
within the salary range based on an assessment of the employee's personal
performance, versatility and skills...

A. The Team Concept...
v. Team members share the responsibility for...
2. rotating jobs within the team...
7. acquiring job knowledge to fulfil all jobs within the team.
8. being a self sufficient team by performing duties previously performed
by other disciplines, e.g. self-inspection, repair, minor maintenance.
9. maintain regular attendance – all share and cover the work of absent
colleagues.
vi. The team involves employees working together as a functional group in
the overall manufacture and assembly of a vehicle.
(Note: the agreement illustrates this with diagrams showing the overlap
between assembly, maintenance and material handling teams and the
integration of manufacturing staff and technical and manufacturing
support in a multi-skilled press shop team.)[31]

increasing willingness to move forward more slowly if the eventual results
for management had a better foundation in more favourable attitudes of
the workforce.[32]

iii. The IDS research concludes that the major demarcations between
craftsmen, and those between production workers and craftsmen are still
very much in place. It may be surprising to trade unionists in industry
that IDS conclude that employers generally have recognised the importance
of respecting craft attitudes and in reality they are adapting working
arrangements to deepen skills.[33] The research between 1981 and 1989 by
Dr Michael Cross is cited in support of IDS' arguments.[34]

The survey by Cross of 236 manufacturing sites shows that 34 per cent
of sites had broken down the demarcation between instrument mechanic
and electrician jobs, compared with 17.5 per cent in 1981. Also, the sites

where the functions of fitters and fabricators were combined numbered 70 per cent in 1989, compared with 40 per cent in 1981. However, as IDS points out, what this represents is a significant consolidation of closely-related craft skills, and not a widespread dismantling of demarcation between the main craft and production jobs.[35] This is further emphasised by Cross's research which shows that the 1981 figure of 95 per cent for those sites which had a clear distinction between maintenance and production functions had only been reduced to 87 per cent by 1989. In addition, his research shows practically no change at all in this area between 1987 and 1989.

Essentially, the evidence suggests that many companies may have learnt to be more realistic by 1990 in terms of the degree of workplace flexibility they can achieve. It is interesting that IDS conclude that, whilst multi-skilling remains an aim for many companies, the more important issue in a wide range of industries is how to build on specific skills within the workplace in order to attain specific objectives, particularly the reduction of down-time.[36]

This observation is of course of interest in light of the importance of reducing down-time to enable the establishment of effective just-in-time production.

iv. The question of training is another issue which is particularly relevant to labour flexibility. IDS conclude that levels of investment in training in UK companies were typically at best only half the levels of their main EU competitors, but there had been some growth in investment levels in training in the UK since the mid-1980s. This factor could give some encouragement to increased functional flexibility of labour.

v. IDS have also reported some interesting findings with regard to the related issues of teamworking and labour flexibility. In 1988 IDS suggested that there had been an increased emphasis on teamworking compared with the position two years previously.[37] If teamworking has become a special focus of attention for management, then the rationale for this could be because of the way in which teamworking can serve several management purposes at once, and typifies particularly well the integrated approach to new management initiatives associated with leading Japanese companies. Teamworking can become an effective vehicle for employee involvement, having significant effects on attitudes of the kind associated with employee involvement philosophy. Teamworking can become an effective vehicle for the problem-solving approaches central to *kaizen* ('continuous improvement') and just-in-time, and can be the basis for updated versions of quality circles. However, the function of teamworking emphasised by IDS is in implementing functional flexibility within the teams, the essential principle being that targets and tasks are laid down for the team to complete, but the team is given considerable discretion in how they are achieved.

vi. IDS reported some interesting observations about teamworking, team leaders and the role of supervision.[38] In spite of the promise, teamworking has posed some problems for management, not least in respect of the role of the team leader. The problem is concerned with reconciling the role of the team leader with the role of the supervisor. In attempts to resolve this problem, a wide variety of definitions of team leader roles have emerged in the UK. An important question often considered by management is whether team leaders should retain any of the disciplinary functions of supervisors. If they do, however, it is doubtful whether the promise of teamworking as a vehicle for the implementation of an integrated programme of new management initiatives can be fulfilled. If supervisory staff make the successful transition from their traditional role to that of team leader, it is more likely that they will have to face the challenge of replacing an authoritarian management style with more discreet forms of leadership. If the team leader adopts a traditional supervisory style of management, this is likely to reinforce the traditional attitudes of the workforce, and frustrate key objectives of teamworking in relation to employee involvement. In addition, autonomous work groups may emerge from teamworking initiatives, with the effective abolition of supervisory functions.

In any case the role and status of supervisory staff have faced an important period of change in recent years. Companies are finding it difficult to get existing employees to adapt to the fact that the front-line manager's role often needs to change more than any other single job. Recruiting high-quality supervisors can be an extremely difficult task for companies.[39]

vii. Labour flexibility trends at greenfield sites are another important issue. 'Full flexibility' appears to be almost entirely restricted to these sites. IDS suggests a link between highly selective recruitment policies at greenfield sites and their success with labour flexibility.[40] Those greenfield sites which have not yet achieved 'full flexibility' appear to continue to make important advances in that direction.

viii. Much of the preceding debate has focused on union agreements to identify the trends regarding functional flexibility. However, this does not provide us with the full picture. There are of course many non-union workplaces where collective bargaining does not occur. In addition, functional flexibility may develop in a workplace as a result of the introduction of new technology. In the absence of a new technology agreement, and in the event of a gradual introduction of new technology, considerable increases in labour flexibility might eventually be established without recourse to negotiation, and perhaps with minimal conflict.

In conclusion, the research by IDS suggests that change towards greater functional flexibility of labour in the workplace has generally been more gradual in the late 1980s than it was in the earlier part of the decade, with most employers in most sectors modifying their expectations of the speed of change. The indications so far are that this pattern is continuing into the 1990s.

Factors which have influenced labour flexibility trends

A range of factors can be identified which appear to have influenced trends in labour flexibility since 1979, some of which have encouraged, some discouraged the trend towards greater flexibility.

i. One important argument is that functional flexibility of labour has been bought by many employers in the 1980s through wage settlements above the rate of inflation. It has been suggested that this is something many employers have been quite willing to do in the *post-1982* climate of rising profitability and productivity.[41] Part of the logic here is that it is better for management to introduce changes in working practices (ie, increased functional flexibility) by agreement, since workforce attitudes are likely to be more positive than if they were imposed. There is also evidence to show that where the cost to the employer of increased functional flexibility has been a wage settlement significantly above inflation, this has often been financed partly from a reduced wage bill as a result of redundancies. In the early 1980s, employers were able to introduce such changes particularly cheaply because of the economic recession of that period.[42] In light of the deeper economic recession of the 1990s, there may be new implications for the cost to employers of flexibility agreements.

ii. In spite of its negative effects on workforce attitudes, the threat of redundancy or closure has been a common weapon used by employers to impose labour flexibility packages since 1979. It was often used in the case of the 'blockbuster' flexibility deals, more common in the earlier part of the decade in most sectors, though spread throughout the decade in the chemicals industry.

iii. The repeal of many workers' legal rights since 1979, which were established through the Employment Protection Act and related legislation of the 1974-79 Labour governments, has been important in enabling employers to extend numerical flexibility in recent years. The introduction by a Conservative government of a requirement of two years employment before any entitlement to many employment protection rights has been a factor in giving employers greater scope to make use of temporary labour.

iv. Skill shortages and under-investment in training relative to other EU countries are two important obstacles to a speedier introduction of functional flexibility. The skill shortages problem can still occur in periods of recession and in areas of high unemployment. It was suggested earlier that there may have been a slight increase in UK employers' expenditure on training since the mid-1980s. However, to catch up with European competitors in respect of investment levels in training demands major additional expenditure, and many companies are paying the price for years of neglect of this issue.

v. The initiatives which UK management have taken regarding labour flexibility since 1979 need to be considered in relation to initiatives on just-in-time production and employee involvement. Certainly a company may take labour flexibility initiatives without having plans for the introduction of just-in-time, but if an employer introduces just-in-time, then it is difficult to develop JIT effectively without extensive functional flexibility, and it may require significant numerical and temporal flexibility as well. So increasing adoption of just-in-time methods by employers can be expected to act as a driving force for increased labour flexibility of one form or another. The relationship of labour flexibility to employee involvement is also important. There is increasing evidence to suggest that the climate for change in terms of workforce attitudes has to be right if management require more than a superficial, short-term form of functional flexibility. Since employee involvement is very much about changing attitudes, about attempts to move away from divisive workplace culture, then an employee involvement programme may lay some kind of foundation for the step-by-step introduction of functional flexibility in the workplace.

Labour flexibility: implications and the trade union response

Flexibility through single union agreements

The introduction of flexibility in the workplace through single union no-strike deals remains the exception in the UK. The fact remains, though, that they are by far the most effective means in the UK of introducing widespread functional, numerical and temporal flexibility of labour outside non-union workplaces. It has been particularly difficult for employers to introduce single union deals at established sites, though it has been done (for example, the Norsk Hydro heavy chemicals site on Humberside).[43] But at established union sites some employers may attempt to undermine joint union structures, and try to tempt workplace unions into separate negotiations. And the purchase of industrial land by employers surplus to their immediate requirements could be an indicator of single union greenfield site plans, particularly if the land is adjacent to established, unionised workplaces at which management have been frustrated in their attempts to introduce an extensive new management techniques programme.

Package deals and the price of functional flexibility

As stated earlier, the price for employers of introducing functional flexibility has varied in the 1980s. In the earlier part of the decade, in the wake of the recession, the prospects for cheap, rapid change looked good for employers. As the decade developed the impact of 'blockbuster' flexibility agreements, whether incorporated in single union deals or not, was not as impressive, and employers had to pay a higher price for the introduction of functional flexibility. This higher price came essentially in two forms: wage settlements above inflation and harmonisation in terms of a shorter working week. Though the price of change may have declined once more with the development of a deep recession in the 1990s, the issues raised for union policy by these package deals, both long term and short term, are important. They may return to the agenda as the 1990s decade unfolds.

It is probably fair to say that there are instances where unions have been defeated or out-manoeuvred by management, and have accepted, with considerable reluctance, the linking of the introduction of functional flexibility to wage rises and/or reductions in the working week. There are other instances, however, both at national and local levels, where unions have been more than willing to adopt a negotiating stance from the start which has deliberately encouraged a trade-off of increased flexibility in return for an above average pay deal or reduction in working hours. This was indeed the original stance of the Confederation of Shipbuilding and Engineering Unions in their national negotiations on the 35 hour week campaign in the late 1980s.

A question for union policy is whether the aim should be to keep negotiations on labour flexibility quite separate from mainstream negotiations on wages and working time. Whilst this is feasible with regard to functional flexibility, it is more difficult to separate a union agenda of a shorter working week, longer holidays, etc., from an employer's agenda of temporal flexibility in terms of averaged and annualised hours, new shift patterns, and associated issues. There is, however, a popular trade union argument that labour flexibility should be kept separate from mainstream negotiations on wages and hours. It suggests that the loss of union influence, deterioration in members' conditions and the threat to jobs in the future will turn out to be a heavy price for which union members will have to pay in future years, in exchange for a pay deal, perhaps soon wiped out by inflation, or for a minor reduction in the working week. The alternative union argument is that it is better to oversee through negotiation the gradual and controlled introduction of some degree of labour flexibility, with a price exacted from employers for it, than to watch helplessly the unfettered, unilateral implementation of widespread flexibility which might occur if a package deal is opposed on principle.

The other important point is that if unions exact a price for increased labour flexibility in terms of a significant reduction in the length of the working week, the implications are different to those where labour flexibility is linked to an above average pay rise. Functional flexibility is intended to bring about increases in productivity, which can lead to job losses. To link the demand for a shorter working week, rather than a pay rise, to increased functional flexibility at least has some potential for off-setting the threat to jobs which increased functional flexibility may pose, provided that a significant reduction in working hours is actually achieved.

Functional flexibility, job satisfaction and training

There are some workers who welcome some of the implications of functional flexibility. It may provide the opportunity of escape from a particularly monotonous job and the chance to develop new skills, providing retraining possibilities perhaps not previously available to older workers. This is the promise of functional labour flexibility. It is of course not always the reality.

If an employer's primary aim in introducing functional flexibility is to increase productivity and to reduce wage costs, then an objective is likely to be to achieve this with a minimum increase in training costs. There is little incentive for employers, in the absence of substantial government subsidies for training costs, to provide training in general transferable skills which can be used in other jobs with other employers. Whilst some retraining will

The main features of TUC policy on flexibility at work

- Unions *welcome* the introduction of new machines and methods that help promote better productivity and efficiency.
- Unions insist on *influencing change* through negotiation and agreement.
- Unions are concerned to encourage change but *not* at the *expense of members' jobs and conditions.*[44]

have to take place to develop functional flexibility, the end result may provide a greater variety of equally monotonous jobs.

Numerical flexibility, workers' rights and union organisation in non-manufacturing sectors

The role of workers' rights legislation, of the kind associated with the employment protection legislation of the 1970s, is important in discouraging the development of numerical flexibility. Labour Party policy advocates the reintroduction of this kind of legislation, in sympathy with the Social Chapter. Numerical flexibility has grown in recent years particularly in the non-manufacturing sectors of the economy, in precisely those areas which are weakly organised in trade union terms or are non-union. Unions like the TGWU have begun to address this question of recruitment in these sectors. Failure to make serious progress towards the resolution of the problem of union organisation in this sector will hamper the implementation of any future legislative programme on workers' rights, and in turn provide employers with continuing opportunities to extend numerical flexibility in these sectors of the economy.

It would be a mistake, though, to ignore other factors which deny employers in non-manufacturing sectors a completely free hand to introduce numerical flexibility. In spite of the economic climate, there are indications that some non-manufacturing sectors (the retail trade, for example) have suffered problems of high labour turnover. Depending on the extent of this problem, the bargaining power of employers in these sectors may not be quite as great as often imagined. However, high labour turnover also creates difficulties for trade union organisation in terms of the retention of membership.

Temporary workers and the union response

As stated earlier in this chapter, where firms operate a high degree of

---

Functional flexibility agreements: possible trade union safeguards

- No redundancies, or if not possible no compulsory redundancies.
- Health and safety considerations to be of prime importance especially regarding training, rather than just tagged onto agreements.
- Training to be provided by public sector institutions leading to NCVQ recognised qualifications together with no restrictions on access such as age or sex.
- Where training is provided on-the-job by other workers, payment of a training allowance.
- No reduction in the number of recognised unions or favoured status to be given to any one.
- Members to have access to shop stewards of their own union on issues like discipline.
- No reduction in the numbers of shop stewards.
- Comparable flexibility changes in the management structure.[45]

---

numerical and functional flexibility, there is evidence to suggest that a distinct line cannot be drawn between an outer group of temporary workers with inferior conditions and little job security, and an inner core of 'permanent' workers on superior conditions and high job security. This conclusion is contrary to Atkinson's flexible firm model. Unions might reasonably conclude, therefore, that the effects on the 'permanent' workforce of the employment of temporary labour are not likely to be essentially different from traditional experiences of temporary labour. The pay, conditions and job security of the 'permanent' workers will probably be undermined by the presence of significant numbers of temporary workers. The dangers for union organisation of a divided workforce, particularly in the event of industrial action, are not difficult to anticipate.

Therefore, an effective trade union response is likely to revolve around the following objectives: the prevention or restriction of increases in the proportion of temporary workers, the establishment of equal pay and conditions for existing temporary and 'permanent' workers, and the incorporation of temporary workers into the 'permanent' workforce. Although such objectives may be difficult for some unions to achieve, partial progress towards them is feasible for unions in spite of unfavourable economic and political conditions.

Other forms of numerical flexibility

Numerical flexibility refers not only to the use of temporary labour, but also to part-time labour and sub-contracting. If job share and career break schemes fail to contain key safeguards for employees, they too may be used by employers to extend numerical flexibility.

i. Part-time working is often a source of cheap labour for employers and often acts to undermine conditions and pay of full-time workers. At the same time there are certain aspects of part-time work which are beneficial to certain groups of workers, particularly women.

Part-time work is also often temporary, and the combined effect of the two means lack of job security, lack of many legal rights, exclusion from occupational pension schemes and denial of bonus, overtime and unsocial hours payments. If part-timers work 16 hours or more per week, then entitlement to the employment protection legal rights of full-time workers comes into force, but employers often make a point of ensuring that contracts maintain hours below this figure. If part-timers work eight hours or more per week continuously for five years or more then they are also entitled to the employment protection rights of full-timers, but again employers often use temporary contracts, or may dismiss part-timers within the five year period in order to prevent this occurring.[46] Part-timers are often disadvantaged in terms of training and promotion opportunities, and sometimes suffer neglect from unions and shop stewards, even in organised workplaces. However, unions are beginning to recognise the increasing importance of union recruitment and organisation of part-time workers.

Part-time work provides the only job opportunity for many women (and some men) with children and other domestic responsibilities. An obvious objective for trade unions is to fight for permanent contracts for part-time work. If unions can make progress on this and the other main disadvantages

---

Possible union objectives for part-time labour

- Hourly wage rates and bonuses equivalent to full-time workers.
- Pro-rata sick pay, holiday pay, maternity pay and pensions.
- Adequate meal breaks and tea-breaks.
- No discrimination in redundancy arrangements.
- Inclusion in training schemes together with opportunities for promotion.
- Premium rates for excess time beyond normal part-time hours together with any shift or unsocial hours payments.[47]

to employees usually associated with part-time labour in the 1990s, then not only will full-time workers feel less threatened by part-time labour, but also the opportunities it could provide, particularly for women workers, could really become worthwhile, rather than simply the only alternative available.

The significant use by employers of part-time labour poses a particularly difficult challenge for unions, but because of the equal opportunities dimension to the issue, if unions manage to meet the challenge, the gains for them in the 1990s in terms of their authority and bargaining power could be considerable.

ii. The use of sub-contractors can also pose a difficult challenge to trade unions. In the public sector in particular, sub-contracting may mean a deterioration in the quality of the work done. If this is the case, it is an obvious target which trade unions are likely to exploit to their advantage, particularly since quality is such a focus of management attention. Sub-contractors may employ non-union labour, but industrial action by the trade unions on site to demand union-labour only contracts may run into legal difficulties, because of the 1982 Employment Act in particular. Conversely, where sub-contractors employ union labour, the unions on site may exercise greater influence over the sub-contracted work, but it is not always easy for unions to avoid inter-union conflict in such situations.

iii. Job-sharing and career break schemes can provide significant opportunities particularly for women workers. Job-sharing can provide the convenience of part-time work combined with the advantages, in terms of pro-rata pay and conditions, of full-time employment. The most common purpose for which career break schemes are used by employees, though not the only one, is by women who wish to take several years off work to care for their children. Career break schemes allow them to return to their previous jobs, often with their pay and grade protected. Normally schemes do not allow a period of absence greater than five years.

Possible union objectives for sub-contracting

- Only union labour allowed on site with facilities for regular card checks.
- The right to scrutinise sub-contractors safety policies and equal opportunities policies in advance.
- The circumstances where sub-contractors may be used to be specified.
- Any increase in the use of contractors to be subject to normal negotiation and combined with job security assurances.[48]

The introduction of job-sharing and career break schemes may also help to avoid compulsory redundancies. In these circumstances, though, unions will want to ensure that those taking up the opportunities under these schemes are not doing so out of fear of redundancy, but welcome them in their own right.

Important opportunities are emerging for unions to negotiate the introduction of career break and job-sharing schemes for two reasons. Firstly, such schemes do provide employers with at least some increase in numerical flexibility of labour, particularly career break schemes. Secondly, employers, especially public sector employers, are keen to demonstrate their commitment to equal opportunities, whether apparent or real. Therefore employers are increasingly unlikely to oppose job-sharing and career break schemes in principle.

Temporal flexibility

i. Shiftworking is set to take on more complex patterns if recent trends continue. Whilst shiftworking suits some workers, the greater demands made of employees by more complex systems are well summed up by Dave Barnes.

> The damaging health effects of shiftworking, particularly night-work, on the body clock or circadian rhythms are well-known especially where the shift pattern involves a rapid change-over which prevents the body adjusting to the change. These can include heart, nervous and digestive disorders, stress and sleep deprivation, in addition to disruption of family and social life. Moreover, shiftworkers (again especially those on nights) tend to suffer from poorer canteen, medical and travel-to-work facilities, limited access to training as well as difficulties in getting involved in union activities.[49]

ii. Averaged or annualised hours arrangements are an important example of labour flexibility, and can provide employers with significant cost savings. A shorter working week and increased holiday entitlement are obvious union objectives which might be fulfilled in exchange for an annualised hours agreement. Free transport during unsocial hours and the provision of, or payment for, child-care facilities as a result of the change to annualised hours are two other conditions which unions might set.

iii. Flexitime can also be an ingredient in employers' temporal labour flexibility strategies. Flexitime, like part-time working, may provide opportunities both for employers to exploit in terms of a more cost-efficient

Possible union objectives on shiftworking

- Restriction of shiftworking to essential operations only and resist attempts to extend it to others simply on the grounds of administrative convenience to the employer.
- The highest shift premiums possible on the principle of the further the departure from normal hours, the higher the pay.
- Consolidation of shift premiums into overtime rates, holiday pay, sick pay and maternity pay.
- Comparable facilities with dayworkers including canteen and medical facilities, access to training, time off in lieu for attending daytime union meetings.
- Shift patterns aimed at minimising disruption to the body clock and social life, and eliminating institutionalised overtime (eg, 5-team rotas rather than 4-team).[50]

deployment of labour and for employees in terms of equal opportunities. However, with most flexitime schemes the balance of advantage generally lies with employees in terms of the improved opportunities for workers to modify their working hours to fit in with domestic and other non-work commitments and activities. Unions can strengthen this advantage by securing the withdrawal of restrictions on when workers can take 'flexidays', and the restriction of the number of key workers who must be present to that which is strictly necessary.[51]

Conclusions

The issues for unions raised by the question of flexibility are not straight forward. First, there is a problem of the definition of the term. Is it labour flexibility which is being referred to, or some other kind of flexibility. The idea of labour flexibility makes more sense when the concepts of functional, numerical and temporal labour flexibility are used. A well-publicised issue concerned with labour flexibility is the concept of the flexible firm. However, there are many serious doubts about whether the flexible firm model does anything to help our understanding of the issues.

The years since 1979 do not show a simple pattern of ever-increasing flexibility of labour in the UK. There are important variations between different sectors of the economy, and the pattern has changed over time in several ways. In the earlier part of the 1980s, employers' expectations were high with 'blockbuster' flexibility deals and single union agreements the focus of attention. The pace of change appears to have slowed considerably since, but it may be on a stronger foundation in management terms.

There is a complex web of factors at both national and workplace levels which trade unions have to take into account in the development of policy, though union policy is more developed in respect of the flexibility of labour than it is with the related employee involvement and just-in-time initiatives of management. This is probably because functional and numerical labour flexibility per se cannot really be described as new techniques; they are only essentially new in that they are adopted by employers as part of an integrated new management techniques package.

All the evidence suggests that flexibility of labour will continue to be a key industrial relations issue in the 1990s, though it is difficult to predict exactly which of several possible directions its development will take. Important factors which will influence this include the depth, length and repercussions of economic recession, and the developments on the political front in the 1990s.

Whatever the developments, the significance of the relationship between labour flexibility and just-in-time philosophy, employee involvement, total quality and teamworking is not likely to disappear. On the contrary, an understanding of the relationship between these different management initiatives is likely, as time goes by, to become increasingly important for the development of effective trade union policy on all of these issues.

Notes

1 Will Hutton, 'Flexible friends?', *New Statesman and Society*, 26.1.90, p15.
2 Klaus Bielstein's research for the TUC is an example of this: Klaus Bielstein, *Flexibility: a Trade Union Approach*, TUC Trade Union Education Department, Sept 1986. His is an interesting approach, which distinguishes between external and internal labour markets of the firm.
3 Tim Webb, then national officer for ASTMS (now MSF), 'Flexibility: the Trade Union Perspective', seminar paper presented to the Institute of Personnel Management National Conference, 17.10.85, p1.
4 'Single union agreements backed' and 'Flexible work "will help staff"', *Financial Times*, 18.10.85.
5 John Atkinson, *The Flexible Firm*, Institute of Manpower Studies, Sussex University, 1985, commissioned by the Employment Department.
6 Unless otherwise indicated, this account is based on John Atkinson, 'Flexibility: Planning for an uncertain future', *Institute of Manpower Studies Review*, vol.1, summer

1985, and presented as a seminar paper, Institute of Personnel Management annual conference, Oct 1985.

7 *Ibid.*

8 *Ibid.*

9 *Ibid.*

10 For example, Anne Pollert, 'The "Flexible Firm": A Model in Search of Reality (or a Reality in Search of a Model)?', Warwick Papers in Industrial Relations No19, Industrial Relations Research Unit, University of Warwick, Dec 1987.

11 *The Myth of the Flexible Firm*, Incomes Data Services Report, No514, Feb 1988, p16.

12 *Ibid.*

13 Anne Pollert, *op cit*, summary.

14 TUC Education, *Flexibility at Work: a workbook for trade unionists*, April 1986, p30.

15 *Ibid.*

16 *Myth of the Flexible Firm, op cit.*

17 Michael Cross, 'Total Productive Maintenance', paper for the North East Maintenance Association 21st annual conference, Nov 1989, referred to in IDS Study No454, March 1990, *Flexibility at Work*, pp2-3.

18 TUC Education, *op cit.*

19 *Ibid.*

20 *Ibid.*

21 *Ibid.*

22 'Single union at Nissan UK plant', *The Guardian*, 23.4.85.

23 Nissan Motor Manufacturing (UK) Limited, 'Agreement and Conditions of Employment', 1.1.87, Para 9.

24 *Flexible Working*, Incomes Data Services Study No407, April 1988, p19. The unions have negotiated some significant amendments to this agreement since 1987.

25 Nissan 'Agreement...', *op cit*, Para 1, 8 and 11.

26 IDS Study No.360 (April 1986), No407 (April 1988), No454 (March 1990).

27 *Ibid.*

28 IDS Study No407, *op cit*, p1.

29 IDS Study No454, *op cit*, p1.

30 IDS Study No407, *op cit.*

31 *Ibid*, pp19-20.

32 IDS Study No454, *op cit.*

33 *Ibid.*

34 Cross, *op cit.*

35 IDS Study No454, *op cit.*

36 *Ibid.*

37 IDS Study No407, *op cit*, p7.

38 *Ibid.*

39 IDS Study No454, *op cit.*

40 *Ibid.*

41 See, for example, John McIlroy, *Trade Unions in Britain Today*, Manchester University Press, 1988, pp207-8.

42 IDS Study No454, *op cit*, p8.

43 See Ian Linn, *Single Union Deals: a case study of the Norsk Hydro plant, at Immingham, Humberside*, Northern College/TGWU Region 10, 1986.

44 TUC Education, *op cit*, p42.

45 Dave Barnes, 'Numerical and Functional Flexibility', Discussion Paper No2, the Employers' New Offensive Conference, organised by the Manchester Employment Research Group for the Confederation of Shipbuilding and Engineering Unions in

the North West, Salford, 17.2.90.
46 In March 1994 the Equal Opportunities Commission mounted a successful challenge in the courts to the discrimination experienced by many part-time workers in respect of restricted employment protection rights.
47 Dave Barnes, *op cit.* Most of this is based on the TUC charter for part-timers.
48 *Ibid,* p5.
49 *Ibid,* pp5-6.
50 *Ibid,* p6.
51 *Ibid.*

Chapter 4

Employee involvement

What is employee involvement?

Employee involvement is a general term used in management circles to refer to the following kinds of initiatives and techniques: quality circles, team briefings, attitude surveys and questionnaires, employers' newspapers and videos, profit-related pay and various profit-sharing and share ownership schemes, including ESOPS (employee share ownership plans), suggestion schemes, various kinds of consultative committees, works' councils, harmonisation of conditions and 'single status' initiatives, joint management-union initiatives on training and employers' ballots. Autonomous work groups and teamworking contain a very important employee involvement dimension to them.

This may seem at first glance a diverse list of management initiatives. There are, however, common threads running through them, these being the following:

- the establishment of more effective means of communication between management and workforce;
- the discovery of ways of allowing the company or organisation to benefit from 'shopfloor expertise' traditionally neglected by management;
- the development of the team concept, and of an increased interest in and identification with the problems of the company or organisation;
- the encouragement amongst the workforce of a more sympathetic view of changes which management perceive as necessary and a greater understanding of the 'unavoidability' of cut-backs and redundancies if they do occur.

The list of employee involvement techniques referred to above is not exhaustive. Some companies may launch special projects of their own, with new titles aimed to impress. Japanese companies in particular will almost certainly continue to develop new techniques intended to meet more effectively the aims of employee involvement (EI).

Understanding the aims and principles of employee involvement as a whole is the key to identifying a particular technique as belonging to EI.

Of course, there are differences between the various employee involvement techniques. There are several ways of trying to make sense of these differences, one of which is to categorise them in the following way.[1]

i. *Financial involvement:* including profit-sharing schemes, profit-related pay and employee share ownership plans (ESOPs).

ii. *Job involvement*: including quality circles, attitude surveys and question-naires, autonomous work groups, suggestion schemes.

iii. *Communication and information*: including team briefings, employers' newspapers and management video presentations.

Another way of making sense of the different forms which employee involvement takes is to look at them like this.[2]

a. *Direct*: the EI techniques in which workers are involved on an individual level rather than through their union representatives. This will include, therefore, methods such as quality circles, in which small groups of workers meet on a regular basis in a particular department to try to solve technical problems with regard to how the work is carried out. It will also include methods such as team briefings, which also operate on the basis of regular meetings of small groups in particular departments, but which are intended as a tool of communication to convey management information to the workforce.

b. *Indirect*: the EI methods in which workers are represented on joint workplace or company committees. The various types of consultative committee are the obvious examples of this. Representatives may be elected through the unions at the workplace, though where there is no union or where employers can achieve it at union organised workplaces, they may be *employee* representatives.

c. *Financial*: including profit-sharing, profit-related pay and employee share ownership plans/ESOPs, as in the previous categorisation.

One value of this latter categorisation is that a pattern emerges of a particular growth of direct and financial forms of EI since 1979, rather than an emphasis on indirect forms of EI.[3]

Is employee involvement different from employee participation?

In a recent Employment Department report on employee involvement no distinction was made between the two terms.[4] However, Bryan Stevens, director of the increasingly influential Involvement and Participation Association, did distinguish between the two in a speech at the Institute of Personnel Management (IPM) conference.[5] He saw the difference in terms of the extent to which managers are prepared to involve employees in decision-making. Stevens has also described employee involvement as being based on recognition of the important role of employees in achieving corporate goals and as a means of winning their commitment, but without making any substantial concessions in terms of the management hierarchy and management's 'right to manage'.[6] He sees participation rather differently.

Employee participation

The company which adopts employee participation can be seen as significantly different to the 'employee involvement company'. Stevens argues that in the case of the former, employees play a more active part in the decision-making process of the organisation. Employee participation conveys a much clearer message that employees have a stake in the company, and that traditional management hierarchies must change as a result. This is not to suggest that management loses control over the ultimate decision, but there are important differences between employee participation and involvement with regard to the process which leads to this.[7]

In Stevens' speech to the IPM conference he made the important point that, while few British organisations want *employee participation*, many have adopted *employee involvement on a voluntary basis*, and others have done neither (referred to by Stevens as the 'People Last' companies).

Involvement, participation, the voluntary approach and the European Union

Stevens' IPM speech highlights another important aspect of this debate which is referred to in the Employment Department's 1989 report on employee involvement.[8] The report makes it quite clear that Conservative governments have favoured a voluntary approach to employee involvement and participation, and states their continuing determination to resist the forms of participation which the European Union are attempting to impose on member states. This clarifies the debate considerably because the European Union generally favours employee participation of a form similar to that defined by Stevens and the Involvement and Participation Association, that is, a form which does not leave management authority entirely unaffected. The 1980 draft Vredeling Directive is an example of the EU's approach. It proposed that companies should be obliged by law to establish procedures to ensure certain forms of consultation and the supply of information to employees. Proposals for the harmonisation of company law in the EU,[9] and the proposals for a European Company Statute published in August 1989 are within the same vein. It is quite clear that the majority of UK organisations do perceive a threat to management's right to manage in the EU's approach to employee participation. Some trade unionists may consider the EU concept of employee participation as no *real* challenge to managerial authority in any case. They may be right.

The control of management decision-making

In light of the debate about the differences between employee involvement and employee participation, it should be emphasised that the question about the control of management decision-making is important in understanding the significance of employee involvement and employee participation in UK industrial relations.

- Employee involvement could be seen as being at the end of a continuum based on the degree of change in the control of management decision-making. EI methods may influence management decision-making but effectively make no impact on the control of management decision-making.
- Next might come employee participation as understood by the EU and Bryan Stevens of the Involvement and Participation Association, this entailing some changes in the control of management decision-making, but not directly attacking management's 'right to manage'.
- A bit further along the continuum might be the concept of industrial democracy as advocated in the 1970s Bullock Report and the 'workers on the board' initiatives of the time.
- Quite a lot further along, at the far end of this continuum is the idea of fully-fledged workers' control and management.

With regard to employee involvement, it might appear at first glance that the basic nature of management decision-making is changed. The example of quality circles as involving workers in decisions they had not previously taken part in might be quoted in support of this. In fact, quality circles tend to operate on the principle of identifying problems, investigating them, coming up with solutions, but then waiting for management's approval. Certainly quality circles carry out tasks previously carried out by management, but whilst there may be significant changes to the role of supervisory management as a result, management's right to veto all quality circle decisions means that the ultimate control of management decision-making remains essentially unchanged.

Autonomous work groups are another relevant example. Essentially, they are small teams within a particular department which are set targets and tasks to be completed within a particular time, but are given considerable discretion about how they achieve them and what decisions they make within the group. Amongst other things, this will probably entail flexibility of working practices. Again any change in the nature of management decision-making is restricted purely to a challenge to the supervisor's authority.

Some of the methods of employee involvement may appeal to some trade unionists because the feeling of involvement may increase job satisfaction and some of the methods appear to give them an opportunity to influence management in the way workers want. *The reality is that, whilst the effectiveness of management decision-making may be improved, the control of such decision-making is left essentially unchanged.* Employee involvement is not a form of industrial democracy or workers' control.

The emphasis in the remainder of this chapter will be on employee involvement rather than employee participation. This seems appropriate in light of the fact that the overwhelming majority of UK organisations which are interested in the issues, appear to be concentrating on employee involvement rather than other forms of (EU style) participation.

Employee involvement

Both ACAS and the Industrial Society are enthusiastic promoters of employee involvement techniques. The Involvement and Participation Association (formerly known as the Industrial Participation Association)[10] also plays a role in promoting employee involvement. The CBI provide an auditing service to employers to encourage the uptake of such techniques, and in fact the 1982 Employment Act has a section about employee involvement. This section of the 1982 Act has provoked little attention from the trade union movement, though the TGWU have commented on it in an interesting pamphlet,[11] and the Post Office have made use of the law in 1988 with regard to UCW (postal workers' union) policy on team briefings. A more recent pronouncement on employee involvement by the Employment Department comes in the form of the 'People and Companies' report (1989), made up mainly of case studies of companies where employee involvement methods operate.

What do employers gain from employee involvement?

So what then are the underlying principles of employee involvement? What do employers stand to gain from the adoption of such techniques? What are the general implications for trade unions?

Focussing on the underlying principles of employee involvement is important because it discourages a piecemeal approach to the range of EI techniques. A debate about team briefings, for example, may be inconclusive and misleading unless it is placed in the context of the broader underlying principles of employee involvement.

The picture is clearer if employee involvement is seen partly as an approach to tackling a basic management problem: that of increasing employee motivation and work performance. Need it be said that this management debate about work performance has been going on for a long time, and can be traced back to the American management practitioner and theorist, F.W.Taylor, in the late nineteenth and early twentieth century.[12] The Taylor school of scientific management emphasised economic incentives, and laid the foundation for time and motion study. Taylorist methods were important to Ford in establishing the first assembly line system immediately prior to the First World War. They are methods which have had a fundamental influence on manufacturing world-wide in the twentieth century, and which have been a powerful management tool in attempts to intensify the pace of work. As the twentieth century developed management theorists increasingly drew attention to the significance of social factors in relation to employee motivation, and initially to the social psychology of the workgroup. Mayo, then Maslow, and later Herzburg and McGregor influenced management thinking significantly. This approach to the theory of employee motivation has developed considerably in recent years. Lately we have also witnessed significant changes in the personnel management function in the UK, with a shift to a broader approach based on human resource management.

One simple though useful way of looking at the links between work performance and the factors, including employee motivation, which influence it, is to see it in terms of a four-way relationship between an employee's ability, motivation, job content and methods, and employee performance, with the latter at the centre of that relationship.[13]

Employee involvement: employees brief managers
A number of forms of employee involvement are intended to improve channels of communication directly between employees and management. Management hope to gain a better picture of how their employees see particular issues, of how they are reacting to particular management initiatives, of how their attitudes are changing over a period of time. Attitude surveys and quality circles are relevant here; though many employee involvement techniques which involve improved feedback from employees to management can be seen as acting to brief management more effectively on the best means to increase profit margins through increased productivity. However, such techniques may also be important in helping management to anticipate the willingness or otherwise of the workforce to stand behind the union and fight management over particular issues. Effective use of certain employee involvement techniques gives management a better idea of what they can and cannot achieve.

Employee involvement: workers' expertise used to solve management problems
Many employee involvement techniques recognise the cost effectiveness of making use of the front-line experience, technical knowledge and awareness of workers of how the job is done in reality. They serve to help management solve problems of quality and efficiency, eliminate waste and raise productivity. In addition, the involvement of workers and supervisors as a team in a particular shop or department in finding solutions to these kinds of problems is a process which usually encourages divided loyalties amongst trade union members and nurtures an identity with management's problems and employers' interests.

Employee involvement: company loyalties versus union loyalties
One of the most important factors common to the full range of employee involvement methods is that they have the potential to undermine the loyalty of workers to their trade union and to encourage workers to identify with the interests of their employer. The Labour Research Department summed up the threat to workers' loyalty to their union posed by employee

involvement techniques. 'When people apply for a job at Toshiba Consumer Products in Plymouth, they are told – "Them" is the competition outside. "Us" is the whole staff of the Company.'[14]

Employee involvement: aimed to weaken workers' resistance to employers' demands?
Employee involvement techniques may help to soften workers' attitudes to employers' demands, and may make such concessions as the acceptance by workers of lower pay rises or redundancies more likely, this being part and parcel of an increased identification with the employer's needs and problems.

Employee involvement: intended to mislead and demoralise trade unionists?
One further factor should not be forgotten with regard to employers' newspapers, letters to employees, attitude survey results, employers' ballot results, video presentations, team briefings, etc (all those employee involvement techniques which are concerned with communicating management information to employees). The factor in question is the effect of such employers' propaganda on the outlook of trade unionists. The publication of the results of an attitude survey of the workforce by management, for example, may mislead union members and undermine their confidence in the union's ability to achieve its objectives in that workplace. There are so many different ways in which the questionnaire may be drawn up, and so many different ways in which the results can be presented. Yet management may present the results as if there were only one interpretation.

Strengths and weaknesses for management of employee involvement
There is evidence to suggest that employee involvement works best for management in workplaces where one of the following conditions apply:

i. trade unions have never been recognised by management and there is little or no union membership there;

ii. unions are recognised but there is no strong tradition of union organisation (in particular, the union organisation has not been very important in influencing the attitudes of the workforce or providing them with information), and management exploits that weakness;

iii. where strong union organisation at the workplace has been crushed in the distant past and the majority of the workforce are no longer particularly influenced by that past (for example, the big workplaces in the car industry in Japan).

There is good reason to believe that employee involvement is not effective when operated alongside openly confrontational styles of management, because it is supposed to be about winning the hearts and minds of the workforce, about changing attitudes.

This may prove to be a significant weakness of British management in their attempts to introduce employee involvement. The managers who are conciliatory one minute and coercive the next appear to have a problem to resolve if they are to be effective on the employee involvement front. This is perhaps related to most UK employers' resistance to more *participatory* techniques and their determination to protect 'management's right to manage'. The net effect on workforce attitudes in well-organised union workplaces would appear to encourage a cynical view of what are seen as management attempts to deceive workers with employee involvement techniques. Many current approaches to employee involvement in the UK may fail because of British management's unwillingness to 'grasp the nettle'. However, the underlying principles of EI will remain a relevant issue for UK management, and certain sections of management may soon soon learn from their mistakes under the pressures of intensified competition and the increased battle for market share in most sectors of the economy.

In fact, the apparent contradiction between employee involvement and confrontational styles of management may provide important opportunities for trade unions to protect independent union organisation at the workplace in the face of the challenge of employee involvement.

Team briefings

Team briefings have been described as,

> ...a system of communication operated by line management based upon the principle of cascading information down the line. Its objective is to make sure that all employees know and understand what they and others in the company are doing and why.[15]

Team briefings normally involve groups of around a dozen employees in one particular shop or section, with a supervisor presenting the brief. The brief is in the form of a talk which lasts no more than 30 minutes, and sometimes considerably less. The intention is that the brief contains some information from senior management but that it emphasises local matters and departmental interpretations of this information which has come from the top. Whilst time may be allowed for brief questions at the end, the aim is to control the agenda fairly tightly and avoid a general debate.

Trade union responses: attendance and participation

Team briefings are intended to be predominantly one-way communication from management to the workforce. They are not aimed to make use of workers' expertise to solve management's problems (quality circles are intended to do that). They are not intended as a means for workers to brief management, ie, feedback from the shopfloor (attitude surveys and quality circles are intended to do that). They are intended to encourage sympathy and loyalty to the employer's interests, which may be at the expense of union loyalties. They are intended to reduce workers' resistance to employers' demands, to suggest that there is no alternative to the employer's interests and view of things. These methods of communication imply an underlying management assumption of convergence of management and workers' interests.

Trade unions might benefit from attendance and participation in team briefings if shop stewards have a clear understanding of management aims in using such techniques, if they have prepared their arguments well and if they are sufficiently skillful to intervene in such presentations to be able to turn them into something quite different from that for which they were intended by management. This can be done in several ways.

i. It is not uncommon for the supervisors and foremen who lead team briefings to be poorly trained (if at all) in the techniques, and do no more than read out the written brief to the workforce. Such lack of training can be exploited, since the supervisor is probably ill-equipped to handle an assertive response to the briefing by the workforce.

ii. This kind of employee involvement technique is intended to be predominantly one-way communication, but a skillful shop steward can move the goal-posts. S/he may insist on discussion and a hearing there and then for the union arguments, in accordance with the participative aims of other employee involvement techniques. If the team briefing leader/supervisor refuses to allow discussion and questions requested by the shop steward, this acts to discredit management's employee involvement programme, and makes the management goal of changing workers' attitudes harder to achieve.

iii. Shop stewards can shift the goal-posts even further by asking key questions (for example, requesting certain kinds of company information) which are clearly concerned with important issues, but are not part of the management's planned agenda for that, or perhaps any other, team briefing. Again, this can put management under considerable pressure. If management prevents discussion of the point, this destroys the notion of democratic participation it intends to convey through an employee involvement programme; if management dodges the issue by postponing discussion of the point to a future meeting, this gives the shop steward ammunition for the future and a chance to affect the agenda of future meetings. Shop stewards have a trade union audience and management have to respond to the steward's intervention in front of her/his members, something skillful stewards can use to considerable advantage.

Provided the shop stewards have the skills and understanding to adopt this approach, it can be effective in the short term, but may cause problems for unions in the longer term.

a. A key question concerns its effects on management. If the shop stewards persist with the approach, then management may respond by providing more effective training for the front line team briefers. On the other hand, if management is influenced by the Tom Peters' philosophy, then they might well let the situation resolve itself and deliberately do nothing.[16] The intended consequence of this is that the supervisors presenting the front line team briefings will eventually respond to the growing pressure they will be under by either quitting their job or, more usually, by developing their team briefing skills in response to the stressful situation they are in. This would be in line with the management strategy of the use of stress as a tool for improving performance. Therefore, an implication of the 'attend and participate' approach for unions could be that the skillful shop steward acts to train up supervisors in team briefing techniques and with no cost to the employer.

b. Another key point for unions of the 'attend and participate' approach is that the union reps and shop stewards must be capable of challenging the format of the team briefings. They must possess the necessary skills and have a clear understanding of management's employee involvement objectives. Whilst the senior union representatives in the workplace might know exactly what they are doing, the other stewards/union representatives may not be able to 'score the goals' when attending their own team briefings. This certainly raises the question of training of stewards to cope with the situation, whether it be formal (through the TUC Education Service or courses run by their own union) or whether it be informal (with the joint stewards committee or branch committee taking responsibility for ensuring that all stewards on the site are up to the task). Of course, the other side of this is that participation in the briefings may sharpen up the shop stewards' skills and understanding, and whilst management may think the briefings train up leaders of team briefings, the situation may also improve the stewards' skills.

Trade union responses: attendance without participation

The intention behind this approach is that shop stewards adopt a watching brief, that they simply attend team briefings to ensure that they know what has been said and only participate in exceptional circumstances. By adopting this approach the shop steward can then answer management's arguments and take up the appropriate trade union points with his/her members at suitable times after the briefing and in the absence of the supervisor who has presented the brief.

This approach has the advantage of protecting the shop steward's independence. Also it may prevent shop stewards who cannot cope with the 'attend and *participate*' tactic from having their authority undermined by the team briefing process. On the other hand, departments where there are stewards or union reps who are poor at communicating and arguing for the trade union case with their members will still be vulnerable.

Trade union responses: boycotting team briefings

If such a policy can gain and retain full support from the union membership, it can face management with some serious problems. It is important not to lose sight of management's objectives in introducing team briefings in the first place. They are about changing workers' attitudes. So management's response to a union policy of boycotting team briefings is critical since it may affect attitudes in precisely the opposite way intended by the team briefings. If team briefings are intended to encourage workers' sympathy with the team concept (ie, that management and the workforce need to work together), then an aggressive and authoritarian management response, demanding that workers attend the team briefings, and threatening them with disciplinary action if they do not, will probably have a very definite effect on workforce attitudes. The traditional confrontational culture of the workplace is likely to be reinforced, and workers' loyalty to their union probably strengthened.

Team briefings at the Post Office

As a result of a decision of their 1988 Annual Conference, the postal workers' union, the UCW, issued an instruction to its members to refuse to attend team briefings.[17] The Post Office responded, not simply by threatening disciplinary action, but by seeking and getting an injunction from the High Court on 13 July that year. The injunction instructed the UCW General Secretary to withdraw the Special Branch Circular, which issued the instruction to members not to attend team briefings. The union complied with the injunction on 14 July, and an earlier UCW decision, that union members should attend in a passive capacity, was reinstated.[18] Clearly such a confrontational approach by the Post Office management must have significantly affected the attitudes of their employees. This situation begs the question of how the Post Office management intended to attain the objectives normally associated with team briefings. Was it based on a view that the UCW did not have the real support of their members on the issue? Was it based on some view that management would achieve the objectives of team briefings in the longer term? Or was the decision a result of management incompetence at a senior level?

Trade union responses: total opposition to team briefings

In certain circumstances, the most effective response for unions determined to defend their independence might be for them to oppose the introduction of team briefings from the outset. There is no reason why unions at workplaces where they have not yet been introduced could not adopt policy in advance which clearly opposes their introduction, and to explain the dangers to the membership based on experience elsewhere. Such an approach would create difficulties for management since they would have to introduce team briefings without agreement and in a climate of conflict over the issue. This would make it harder for management to achieve the objectives of team briefings, and would be an important deterrent. Such a policy and programme of education amongst the membership might be a part of a broader policy position for workplace union committees to adopt on employee involvement as a whole. However, whilst trade unionists may be prepared to boycott team briefings as a tactic, there have to be serious doubts about the extent to which union members in some sectors would support an approach of total opposition from the outset.

Weaknesses of team briefings

Team briefings have a number of significant weaknesses. Mick Marchington has referred to several of these.[19]

- Because of the way some workplaces are organised, there may be difficulties in bringing groups together for team briefings on a regular basis and as part of an efficient system – for example, where there are complex shift patterns, where people do most of their work off-site, where there is continuous production.
- The task expected of the supervisor who presents the brief could be very demanding, and that means that effective, on-going training of the supervisor may be critical. There is reason to believe that management often underestimate these training demands.
- The information supplied in the briefing needs to be new and needs to mean something and have some relevance to the workforce. If it does not, the briefings will quickly degenerate, demoralise the supervisor, encourage the workforce to perceive them as the presentation of more management propaganda and fail in their objective of encouraging team attitudes.
- Managers are keen to talk about workplace culture, that is, the set of attitudes, views, opinions, beliefs, and ways of doing things which are all a part of the industrial relations at a particular workplace. The success of team briefings will depend quite considerably on the 'cultural history' of workplaces where they are introduced. A history of distrust and overt conflict between management and unions is not likely to be fertile ground for new management initiatives such as team briefings.[20]

Team briefings are a common employee involvement technique in the UK, in both manufacturing and the public sector. The Industrial Society, in association with the Institute of Personnel Management and the Involvement and Participation Association, have put considerable energy into promoting them, and government departments are only too keen to advocate the idea alongside the other employee involvement techniques.[21] However, it is clear that management will not have an easy path to tread in their attempts to introduce team briefings.

Quality circles

Quality circles are based on regular meetings normally in the employer's time of small groups of workers, of usually less than ten in number and made up of people who work closely with each other in the same shop or department. They meet frequently, sometimes once a week, with a circle leader, often the supervisor, who guides the discussion. Membership of the circle is voluntary. The early quality circles did indeed use such meetings to solve quality problems, whereas they have now come to be used to solve a wide range of work-related problems in addition to quality. Cost-cutting proposals through changes in working methods, stock reduction and the elimination of waste are common projects for quality circles. The quality circle programme is likely to be linked together through a management steering committee with a management-appointed facilitator or co-ordinator. Training is an important dimension of quality circles. The Labour Research Department sees quality circles as groups concerned with solving work-related problems and making recommendations, but seldom having much authority for implementing change.[22]

Quality circle techniques

Quality circles identify a particular problem as a project on which the group will concentrate over several weeks or months. They make use of various problem-solving techniques, usually one or more of the following.[23]

i. *Cause and effect analysis.* This is basically a systematic means of identifying all possible causes of a problem by analysing four factors in turn: manpower, machines, materials and methods.

ii. *Brainstorming.* A well-known training technique in which each quality circle member states at random all the possible causes of the problem she/he can possibly think of until a comprehensive list for the group is drawn up.

iii. *Pareto analysis.* This is a method for drawing out the one or two key causes of the problem from the many possible or secondary causes. Graphs are used for the purpose.

iv. *Force field analysis.* This looks at the pressures or forces in favour of a particular change needed to solve a problem and contrasts these with the obstacles to that change. It may turn out that there is just one main obstacle, for example, a particular individual's attitude.

Trade union responses: attendance and participation

A trade union response to quality circles of 'attend and participate' has more complicated implications for unions than such an approach does with team briefings. Quality circles may produce changes in working practices without negotiation through the unions, and have the effect of producing significant cost savings without financial reward to the workforce. Therefore, any trade union plans to adopt an 'attend and participate policy' will need to take into account the following if they are to be effective.

i. Pay and conditions issues traditionally negotiated by the unions will need to be omitted from quality circle agendas.

ii. All quality circle proposals which result in other changes in working practices will need to be dealt with through the established negotiating machinery.

iii. Assurances will be needed that there will be no threat to jobs or loss of job status as a result of quality circle projects and proposals.

iv. Shop stewards/union representatives will need the right to attend, preferably as and when they think fit as part of a union monitoring process.

v. The financial value of management gains should be forwarded to the established negotiating committee.

vi. Any financial share in benefits should be agreed through the established negotiating committee.

Trade union responses: boycotting quality circles

If management have already begun to introduce quality circles in the workplace, without negotiation, then workplace union committees may face difficulties in retaining the full support of the union membership if they adopt a boycott policy. These problems are likely to stem from the features of quality circles which are attractive to employees.

An effective boycott policy will only have a chance of working if the workplace union committee has carried out a sound programme of education amongst the union membership, explaining the seductive nature of quality circles, and making the dangers to independent trade unionism clear. The dangers include the following:

Attractive features of quality circles: an American worker's experience at General Motors

Like all such programmes it seemed to be confirming what workers have long known, but management have always denied, that the men and women on the shopfloor know best. There were other attractions too – meetings during working hours (being paid to sit around and talk!), a chance to air grievances, participation on a voluntary basis only, prizes for money-saving suggestions, and a feeling that at last management were stopping treating workers like morons.[24]

- that management are trying to make use of shopfloor expertise for nothing;
- that quality circles will not change the control of management decision-making;
- that the authority of shop stewards and the established negotiating structures are potentially threatened.

However, the membership may accept and understand all these points, but still go for the 'attend and participate' strategy, on the basis of a controlled, negotiated introduction of quality circles, perhaps in restricted areas of the workplace or on a pilot-scheme basis.

Trade union responses: total opposition to quality circles

Unions at the workplace may oppose the introduction of quality circles from the beginning, and refuse to negotiate on the issue. Management then have to take the decision of whether to introduce them unilaterally or to put the issue on ice. If the union takes a total opposition stance it will probably have problems in maintaining it unless it has carried out a thorough educational campaign amongst the membership on the issues of the kind already referred to. Management will introduce quality circles unilaterally where they are confident that that they can drive a wedge between the workplace union committee and the union membership, or where there is no recognised union in any case. Management have some powerful arguments in their favour in support of quality circles, and incidences are common where union committees have the trappings of strong organisation but, having neglected the campaigning and educational work and effective communication with the membership over the years, have proved incapable of effective opposition.

TUC and TGWU on quality circles

The TUC made a important contribution to the early debate on quality circles with a significant statement in 1981. It has not followed this through in the years since with any extensive debate explaining the links between quality circles and the other employee involvement techniques, and/or explaining the way they relate to other management initiatives such as the various forms of flexibility and just-in-time production. Nevertheless, the 1981 TUC policy statement on quality circles is still worth consulting.[25]

In 1984 the TGWU General Executive Council responded to the issue, and, following a period of debate involving the union's National Trade

Groups and a visit by the ACTSS National Secretary[26] to the Ford Motor Company's sites in the USA to look at their employee involvement programme, the TGWU published a useful pamphlet on the subject.[27] This outlined the nature of the policy debate within the union. It states that there was unanimous opposition amongst the Trade Groups to the introduction of quality circles, but that there were also dangers that they might be introduced in workplaces without union control of the situation, and that whether the union liked it or not, they already existed in some workplaces. The pamphlet concludes by emphasising the General Executive Council's warning of the dangers of quality circles. It urges shop stewards and union officers to establish a clear policy on these issues at a workplace level, to present a strong position to management and warns of the dangers to members' rights and conditions of a complacent or wait and see approach to these issues.[28]

The TGWU developed their policy on employee involvement and quality circles through an extensively revised edition of this pamphlet published in 1989.[29]

Quality circles: weaknesses and strengths for management

Quite a lot of the early quality circles in the UK failed, and quite a number of employers associated with these failures have had to resurrect quality circles under a different name, or to pursue the objectives of quality circles through other employee involvement methods and management initiatives. A common error of management appears to have been to see quality circles as *the key* to Japanese business success, rather than as one of several

Origins and history of quality circles

Quality circles are commonly associated with Japanese new management techniques, but the early ideas originated in the United States. The ideas of American management specialists Deming and Juran, in conjunction with the work of Professor Ishikawa, were first put to practical effect through the establishment of quality circles in Japan in the 1960s.

In the mid-1970s American companies like Lockheed, General Motors and Honeywell developed the first examples of quality circles in the West.

By the late 1970s British companies were beginning to show an interest; Rolls-Royce Aero Division has claimed to be the first in 1978. Estimates suggest that 100 companies in the UK by 1981, and 400 by 1985, had introduced quality circles.[30]

ingredients of a new kind of management philosophy and practice. They were often introduced in a climate of desperation in the face of intense foreign competition and battles for market share. It seems that they were often introduced without adequate planning and finance, and promoted by a tier of middle management keen to make a name for itself, whilst lacking the support for, or understanding of, the issue by senior management. But certainly, there is evidence to suggest that the biggest single reason for the disintegration of quality circles was in fact redundancy and/or company restructuring caused by the economic situation.[31]

In spite of these problems for management, it would be a mistake to consider the debate about quality circles as no longer important. For all those that have failed, many have been established successfully in management terms. Managers have learnt something from their mistakes. Quality circles are developing in France, Germany and Italy, as well as the UK, USA and Japan. They may be modified to suit local circumstances, or emerge under new names. The fact remains that from a management stance, the essential method still has potential. That potential is closely associated with the kinds of points made by the American worker at General Motors, quoted earlier. There is an aspect of quality circles which may well appeal to union members. There is a greater *feeling* of control, although in reality control and influence over significant management decisions is likely to be minimal.[32] Whether management in the UK will realise that potential remains to be seen. It will depend considerably on their understanding of the issue, their skill and competence. It will also depend on the policy, tactics and vigilance of trade unions at both national and workplace levels.

Attitude surveys

Attitude surveys entail the use of questionnaires, often organised by consultants who are brought in to act on behalf of management. The questionnaires are distributed to the workforce to ascertain workers' views on various issues. The issues might range from general questions about workplace morale and pride in the job to standards of communications within the organisation and opinions about pay and conditions. The results of these surveys are then often presented to the workforce in a simplified form, with the use of graphs and selected comments, in a special edition of the company newspaper.

Results of an attitude survey at a well-known truck company

The results were presented in a glossy broadsheet edition of the company newspaper, with the following conclusions being given prominence and presented by means of pie charts and graphs.[33]

	Agree	Disagree
'I am proud to work for Leyland Daf'	92%	8%
'Unless we become more competitive we won't survive'	92%	8%
'I feel I could make a greater contribution to Leyland Daf's success'	66%	34%

	Strongly agree	Agree	Disagree
'Leyland Daf's most important goal is quality'	41%	45%	14%

	Major preferred source	Minor preferred source	Not a preferred source
'My immediate supervisor/manager is my preferred source of information'	68%	24%	9%

What might management gain from attitude surveys?

Attitude surveys are intended to provide feedback directly from the workforce, with employees apparently having their say. The results may suggest something different to the views being expressed by the union on their behalf. The survey results may imply that management knows the feelings of the workforce better than the union does, with the claim by management that the survey is an expression of direct democracy.

i. Attitude surveys are one component in a programme of employee involvement. This aims to establish a system which briefs management much more accurately than in the past about the mood of the workforce in respect of what it may and may not be prepared to accept.

ii. Attitude surveys are intended to promote company loyalty, step by step. If they are successful in this it is usually at the expense of union loyalty. Management advocates of attitude surveys argue that if employees desert the union in these circumstances then so be it since they are simply exercising their free choice. Two things are significant in this respect, these being the restriction of survey questions to the company's problems, and the evidently common practice of aggressive publicity of results which are favourable to the company's viewpoint.

iii. Attitude surveys may be used as a tool to ease in other employee involvement techniques. For example, if the survey results suggest that the vast majority of employees want more information about the company's financial position, this might be used as an argument to support the introduction of team briefings. If the survey results suggest that the majority of employees see quality as a key issue for the company, this may be used as an argument to support the introduction of total quality systems.

Trade union responses: do nothing?

Some union workplace committees have argued that an organised union reaction to attitude surveys is unnecessary. This is based on the view that attitude surveys and the publication of their results are a part of management and company propaganda, but that union members are not likely to be deceived by them, that in any case attitude surveys are probably only a passing management fad, and for unions to make a serious effort to oppose attitude surveys is a distraction from much more important issues which they face in the workplace. Attitude surveys may not have much immediate impact in themselves, but there is the fact that they are a component of a broader programme of employee involvement, with management intent on moving forward, step by step, towards the longer term objective of significantly changing workplace culture. That objective is very important to management if it is to succeed with its labour flexibility programmes, just-in-time production, total quality and teamworking initiatives. If unions adopt a *long term* 'do nothing' strategy with regard to attitude surveys, they may experience a gradual erosion of the union loyalty of members in the workplace.

Trade union responses: exploiting survey weaknesses

Management questionnaires and survey results can be vulnerable to closer, critical scrutiny, particularly in respect of the following points.

i. The basis for the choice of questions might be challenged by unions. A high proportion of survey questions are likely to be related to current management campaigns, and this probably compares unfavourably to the number of questions which represent the broader, unrestricted concerns of unions and employees about the workplace and the conditions of employment.

ii. Questions and the words used in them may be loaded. For example, it is difficult to say no to the question 'Are you particularly concerned about quality?'

iii. The questionnaire may not allow employees to answer questions in the way they want, by limiting responses to two or three short, given answers and preventing elaboration. For example, the real answer to the question, 'Are you proud to work for company X?', could be an enthusiastic 'yes' in certain respects, and a hostile 'no' in others.

iv. Management may produce a selective presentation of the survey results. If the results are published in the company newspaper, then an editing process will inevitably occur. Management will make decisions about which aspects of the survey results will be given prominence, and therefore what will hit the headlines in the company newspaper. If the survey has produced one or two embarrassing results for management, it is difficult to see how this could fail to influence management decisions about the nature of publicity. Management are potentially vulnerable to trade union exploitation of these factors.

v. A way in which any survey results can be manipulated is to distort the significance of the percentage of people who give a particular answer to a question by ignoring the percentage who replied to the questionnaire. Another is to fail to distinguish between significant groups in the survey. For example, 70 per cent of the workforce might be very enthusiastic about quality circles, but this may hide the fact that the shopfloor are totally behind the idea, whilst the white collar staff are overwhelmingly hostile to it.

If unions in the workplace do manage to exploit these areas of management vulnerability, then a prerequisite of this is an effective system of communication between the workplace union committee and the union membership to get these points across. A joint shop stewards committee or union branch bulletin may play an important role in this respect.

Trade union responses: boycotting attitude surveys

If unions in the workplace are opposed to attitude surveys, they may gain from discouraging the completion of questionnaires by their members. A low response to the questionnaire makes management publicity of the survey results vulnerable to effective union criticism in respect of the survey's statistical validity, and management's credibility regarding its employee involvement programme may be damaged as a result. However, if unions are determined to oppose attitude surveys a boycott alone is unlikely to be sufficient.

Trade union responses: a union attitude survey

This is one tactic which, if developed by unions at the workplace, could turn out to cause considerable problems for management's use of attitude surveys. The adoption of this approach by unions at British Aerospace is interesting.[34] One effective method is to draw up and distribute the union questionnaire at the same time as that being carried out on behalf of the employer (probably by management consultants). The key for unions is to ensure that the questions in their survey reflect the issues the unions believe their members are really concerned about. Also, the way in which the results are communicated to union members is important. In the case of the British Aerospace union survey a local trade union research organisation was used. Such an organisation may be able to do a computer analysis of the results and present them in a professional report format for the unions.[35] This parallels the use of management consultants by the employer for their survey. An effective union tactic would be to circulate widely the union survey report, with union representatives drawing the attention of union members to the results. Such a report could prove useful for workplace unions in the future: when management are keen to quote their survey results to justify a particular initiative, the unions will be in a position to respond by quoting their own survey results.

The principle behind this type of trade union response is for unions to employ essentially the same techniques against management in organising a union attitude survey as management have employed against the unions in organising theirs. Well-organised, a union response of this kind could cause considerable difficulty for management, potentially neutralising the effects of management attitude surveys.

Employee involvement: the communication element

Attitude surveys and quality circles have a communication element to them. Team briefings are about direct communication downwards from management to employee. Other employee involvement methods which are intended to perform a similar communication function include video presentations, company newspapers, management circulars and personal letters to employees. Communication is not the sole element of employee involvement, but it is an important part of it. This element of employee involvement poses a challenge to the effectiveness of communication between the trade union organisation in the workplace and union members.

Shop stewards and union representatives at some workplaces may be convinced that their union organisation is strong compared with others in their area or industry, based on apparent evidence in terms of relatively high wage rates and good conditions, and perhaps impressive trade union time off and facilities agreements. Such factors are unreliable indicators of the strength of union organisation in the workplace. When faced with a well-organised, assertive employee involvement programme, perhaps quickly introduced, it may be that shop stewards and union representatives in such workplaces have difficulty in retaining membership support for the key union issues. If this occurs the explanation may be connected with the following factors.

i. It may be that the good pay, conditions and union facilities have not been fought for by the union over the years – they have in fact been given by management as a means of discouraging the emergence of union militancy. The consequence of this may be that the union representatives in the workplace have actually had little experience of serious conflict with their employer, and tend towards a conciliatory approach in their relationship with management.

ii. It may be that the system of communication between union representatives and members has actually been weak for years in that particular workplace, and a complacency has set in, with union representatives believing that they are doing a good job and members not doing too much about the lack of communication for the same reason, that is that pay and conditions are good relative to other workplaces.

A workplace with this kind of history usually provides management with encouraging opportunities for the implementation of an effective employee involvement programme.

Union communication with members

Even if the unions at the workplace have won good pay, conditions and union facilities through hard struggle, an effective system of communication between union representatives and members is essential for unions if they hope to retain membership loyalty when faced with management information supplied to their members through employee involvement techniques. With the challenge of sophisticated, well-planned employee involvement programmes, the effective protection of trade union independence in the workplace will depend significantly on the extent to which unions are prepared to assess their existing methods of communication and to update and improve them. Since management will increase the volume of written information they distribute to employees as a result of employee involvement programmes, unions at the workplace are likely to gain from increasing the volume of their printed information to union members. Whilst union leaflets and posters have always been important tools for unions, a union bulletin with plenty of local information in it about that particular workplace can substantially improve union channels of communication with members. Unions in the workplace are also likely to gain in these circumstances from a careful review of the communication skills and performance of their shop stewards and union representatives, linked to a trade union education programme which is aimed to improve this critical, direct and personal channel of communication with the union membership.

EI as financial involvement

Financial employee involvement methods are an attempt to involve workers in the financial successes and failures of the company, and typically take the form of profit-sharing schemes, profit-related pay and employee share ownership schemes. Such arrangements are not new, but employers have certainly shown a renewed interest in them in the 1980s, to the extent that nearly 25 per cent of companies had some kind of scheme established by 1985.[36] This has been partly stimulated by the Finance Acts of 1978, 1980 and 1984.

Profit-related pay
Profit-related pay systems link a certain proportion of employees' pay to variations in company profits. The 1987 Budget introduced tax relief to encourage this. The Conservative government saw the main aims of profit-related pay as helping to break down the 'them and us' divisions in British industry, and encouraging more flexible wage systems which might contain some of the impact of recession in terms of redundancies.[37]

Profit-related pay can be interpreted as an element of a much broader trend away from wage payment systems based on the rate for the job. One of the consequences of this trend is to reduce the power of unions to negotiate on pay and conditions. It is also a part of a trend in certain sectors of employment to replace collective bargaining with individual employee negotiation on pay and conditions. The elements of the process in addition to profit-related pay include the following.

i. Merit payment systems and performance-related pay, particularly in white-collar occupations and the public sector. Such payment systems are also driven by management objectives of simultaneously cutting wage bills and increasing productivity.

ii. The growth of individually negotiated contracts of employment.

iii. Widespread attempts by employers, notably in the public sector, to replace national collective bargaining units with local bargaining units.

iv. These developments can be related to the broad shift in emphasis in British society, promoted by successive Conservative governments, away from collectivism and towards individualism. Whether this is of a temporary or more permanent nature is a matter of debate.

Profit-sharing schemes

Depending on the recent financial performance of the company, profit-sharing schemes distribute a proportion of profits to the workforce, whether in the form of shares or cash. Many companies take the view that profit-sharing schemes are non-negotiable with unions. However, there can be complications for management in introducing such schemes. Schemes are probably more likely to succeed in companies which see them as part of a broader employee involvement programme and philosophy. Rather than changing workplace culture in themselves, such schemes may help to reinforce a participative culture which already exists.[38]

As with other share-based schemes, profit-sharing may increase employees' interest in the financial position of the company, but it does not follow that it will increase employee motivation and lead to increased performance. Not many employees are likely to believe that working harder will necessarily lead to increased profits, and increased profitability may occur without increased performance.

Workplace unions may perceive profit-sharing as a challenge to them if it is introduced as a component of a long-term employee involvement programme. They may also take a critical position because the introduction of profit-sharing is likely to reduce the proportion of the pay packet which they are able to negotiate annually. However, where schemes are introduced, union members may simply 'take the money and run'.

Employee share ownership plans (ESOPs)

Management buy-outs have happened to a number of companies in recent years. Employee share ownership plans can be described as an attempt to extend the buy-out principle to the workforce as a whole. Since the workforce as a whole are unlikely to have the money to buy the company they work for, ESOPs allow the setting up a trust to borrow the money on behalf of the workforce. As the loan begins to be paid off, shares are allocated to employees. Also, at some future date, employees are allowed to sell shares allocated to them, but any shares sold will be bought back by the ESOP.

ESOPs have been about for some time in the USA, and by 1985-86 there were 8000 companies organised as ESOPs, representing 8 per cent of the total US workforce.[39] Management motives for their introduction in the USA are related to significant tax concessions and increased employee motivation. In the UK the trade union Unity Trust Bank is generally acknowledged as the leading expert, and it has acted as advisor to the vast majority of ESOPs when they were set up.[40] (It is also interesting to note that the Unity Trust Bank has advised about ESOPs to teams visiting the UK from Poland, Hungary and the former Soviet Union. The Hungarian and Soviet visits were organised by Job Ownership Ltd and Partnership Research Ltd.)[41]

ESOPs are not workers' co-operatives. In some circumstances they can give the workforce a significant degree of control over the enterprise, but often the balance between the share-holdings of senior managers, obtained through a management buy-out element in the arrangement, and the share-holdings of the workforce are such that the latter have minimal power to influence the direction of the company or important management decisions. A further dimension to this is the possibility of a 'financial coup' which may be organised discreetly by senior management through the management buy-out element of the arrangement. In addition, the make-up of the board of trustees is an important issue, and trade unions may have little influence or representation here. However, the very concept of ESOPs raises questions about employee involvement objectives. ESOPs mean that union members are also share-holders, and so competition between union and company loyalties may emerge. If senior management are able to organise a full employee involvement programme and decide to do so in conjunction with the establishment of the ESOP, this could challenge the influence of the unions at the workplace. The *real* strength of union organisation at that workplace will then be tested.

There are several arguments, then, that indicate a number of complications and common problems for unions organised in workplaces where

ESOPs operate. Where management wish to introduce an ESOP, they may put the argument that there is no viable commercial alternative, and propose that an ESOP be adopted along the lines of one they have already studied at a particular company. Experienced shop stewards and effective workplace unions are likely to resist this *fait accompli* approach. It may be that, after careful consideration, the unions decide to agree to the formation of an ESOP. It may be correct that there is no confident financial alternative to an ESOP, but this does not preclude unions from negotiating the particular form and structure which the ESOP might take. On the other hand, unions may uncover a rather different picture to that painted by management, and oppose the ESOP. In conclusion, the effectiveness of the trade union response to ESOPs would seem to depend significantly on the following factors.

i. Unions are likely to gain from the extent to which they are in a position to reduce the pace of negotiations, in order to provide sufficient time not only to examine the common management argument that there is 'no commercial alternative' to the particular plan proposed by management, but also to look at the proposed ESOP structure and to draw up a list of conditions which might make the ESOP acceptable to the unions.

ii. The management buy-out proportion will be a key factor within the ESOP. It should be kept to a minimum to maximise the control and influence of the workforce as a whole.

iii. Unions will be more effective if they can analyse the management buy-out element to check for a possible financial coup by senior management.

iv. Unions will gain from strong union representation on the board of trustees.

v. Unions may find it easier to maintain the support of their members if they are able to prevent the introduction of a a full-scale employee involvement programme which may be launched alongside the ESOP.

Other forms of employee involvement

Harmonisation

Similar to staff status and single status, this refers to the creation of increasingly similar employment conditions for staff and shopfloor, or management and non-management grades. This process has developed slowly but steadily in the post-war period, with some quickening of pace in the early 1970s and again in the 1980s. It has been suggested that new technology initiatives, the effects of various workers' rights legislation and the removal of legal restrictions on cashless pay have all encouraged harmonisation.[42] However, harmonisation cannot be separated from the factors which have encouraged the introduction of employee involvement programmes. Whilst recession and intensification of competition have stimulated management interest in furthering co-operative attitudes and employee commitment, traditional workplace divisions are likely to subvert such objectives.[43] Three key objectives of employers for the introduction of harmonisation have been suggested by Duncan:[44]

i. to increase labour productivity

ii. to simplify administration and achieve resultant cost reductions

iii. to change employee attitudes, thereby improving cooperation, motivation and morale.

With regard to the implications of harmonisation, they are somewhat ambiguous both for trade unions and employers. Manual unions are likely to want the superior conditions of staff or management grades. At the same time, the approach of management to harmonisation can be selective; cost saving initiatives such as cashless pay and the change from weekly to monthly pay may be given priority. An important point is that the employee involvement element of harmonisation, that is the objective of changing employee attitudes, will mean immediate costs to employers, whilst bringing benefits only in the longer term.

The evidence suggests that there are costs and benefits of harmonisation to both unions and employers. As a result, both unions and management are usually reluctant to negotiate a *comprehensive* harmonisation package, and generally adopt a more cautious, step-by-step approach. An important exception to this are the harmonisation elements of greenfield site agreements.

Indirect forms of employee involvement

The focus of this chapter has been on *direct* forms of EI (team briefings, quality circles, etc) and *financial* forms of EI,[45] because it is these which have been prominent in the management initiatives of recent years. Indirect forms of EI are intended to involve workers through union or employee representatives on joint consultative bodies of various kinds, including works councils. Such consultative structures are fairly common in both the private and public sectors, particularly the latter, and are not a recent development. As a result, where unions are well-organised in the workplace and not isolated from other workplaces, these structures do not appear to have had any significant effect on undermining trade union influence.

This appears to be related to the application of the following principles by unions in well-organised workplaces.

i. The dividing line between negotiation and consultation has been clearly maintained.

ii. Consultation has not been allowed to become a substitute for negotiation.

iii. Unions have prevented management from using consultative forums for negotiating purposes.

Whilst indirect forms of employee involvement are given less prominence at present by management than direct and financial forms, are certain new trends emerging?

i. It is common practice with greenfield site agreements to emphasise consultative structures at the expense of negotiating structures, and sometimes for the former alone to be established. A works council or advisory board, perhaps by another name, will often be part of the agreement. The number of Nissan-style greenfield sites has increased in the UK.

ii. With established sites, where workplaces have no union or a low percentage of union membership, management may set up consultative committees, inviting the election of employee rather than trade union representatives.

iii. Where unions are weak or shop stewards inexperienced, management may attempt increasingly, step-by-step, to substitute consultation for negotiation, and link this to a broader employee involvement programme which they are implementing.

However, recent research published by the Policy Studies Institute casts doubts on the popular arguments which suggest these trends.[46]

Conclusions

There is a strong argument to suggest that employee involvement does pose a significant challenge to the traditional influence of trade unions in the workplace. Employee involvement programmes provide an alternative source of information, of ideas and interpretation of workplace experiences, an alternative to that provided by the union. EI programmes actively promote a new culture in competition with the traditional explanations and culture communicated by the union. In response, unions may adjust or change the message to their members, or perhaps more significantly their methods of communicating. A key issue for trade unions is how to respond to EI initiatives without compromising union independence from management and employer.

It is important that employee involvement should be viewed as a whole and particular techniques should be assessed with respect to how they are related to broader management aims for overall employee involvement programmes. For example, if attitude surveys or team briefings are being introduced in a particular workplace, both management's initiative and the union response will be weak unless they fail to take into account the way in which the various components of an employee involvement programme fit together and serve key EI principles. Both unions and management will also have to give consideration, if they are to operate effectively, to the difficult question of whether there is a contradiction between the EI objective of encouraging a team outlook and the divisive effects of confrontational styles of management. If such a contradiction does exist, unions may have significant opportunities to strengthen their bargaining power in the situation. If it does exist and management fail to find a way of resolving the contradiction in the UK, it could be critical in causing the failure of management EI programmes.

However, there is not only the question of relating particular EI techniques to the overall EI programme and philosophy. Employee involvement needs to be related to the broader context of management initiatives on just-in-time production, labour flexibility, total quality, teamworking, the implications of single union agreements in the UK, and the history and significance of confrontation between leading employers and independent trade unionism in Japan.

To introduce just-in-time, total quality systems, labour flexibility or any other major changes in working practices, management must address the question of workers' attitudes, of *workplace culture*. At Nissan and Toyota in early 1950s Japan, the employers achieved this through inflicting a crushing defeat on the independent trade unions, purging the workplaces with mass sackings of labour movement activists and sympathisers, and establishing company unions. This placed these employers in a powerful position to create gradually a new climate, a new workplace culture, relatively divorced from the past. In fact, these employers seem to have found a way, at least in the context of the car industry in Japan, of resolving the apparent contradiction between EI initiatives and confrontational management methods. With Japanese companies in the UK, greenfield sites have provided the opportunity for no-strike single union agreements, which have also placed management in a relatively strong position to establish a new, *unitary* workplace culture from the start and to launch a *comprehensive* employee involvement programme. Many UK employers have neither of these opportunities available to them, but recognise their need to seize such opportunities if they arose. Companies which demonstrate a pattern of buying land adjacent to their established workplaces may be developing contingency plans in relation to future possibilities for establishing greenfield sites for part of their operation.

Short of such opportunities, employers with union-organised workplaces in the UK will have less fertile soil in which to plant the seeds of employee involvement and a new workplace culture. However, for as long as management needs to make radical changes of the kind associated with just-in-time, labour flexibility, total quality and teamworking, it will return repeatedly to its need to make radical changes in workplace culture. Management may improve its level of ability to introduce employee involvement techniques considerably as time goes by, through the lessons of its experience and perhaps through increased funding for management training and education.

Notes

1 D.Farnham and J.Pimlott, *Understanding Industrial Relations*, Holt, Rinehart and Winston, 3rd edit, 1986, pp70-71.

2 Mick Marchington, 'Employee Participation', in Brian Towers (ed), *A Handbook of Industrial Relations Practice*, Kogan Page and IPM, 1987, pp163-164.

3 *Ibid*, p164.

4 Employment Department Group, *People and Companies – Employee Involvement in Britain*, HMSO, 1989, p4.

5 'Europe – an opportunity to resolve the debate over employee involvement or participation', Special Report on the Institute of Personnel Management annual conference, Harrogate, 1990, *Employment Gazette*, December 1990, p597.

6 Bryan Stevens, 'Employee Involvement or Participation? The Ingredients for Success', *The Personnel Managers' Yearbook, 1989*, AP Information Service Ltd,1989.

7 *Ibid*, p41.

8 Employment Department Group, *op cit*, pp8-13.

9 The European Union's Fifth Company Law Directive.

10 Director: Bryan Stevens. Founded in1884. Address: The Involvement and Participation Association, 85 Tooley Street, London SE1 2QZ. It is worth requesting an up-to-date list of affiliates. It is also worth checking the interesting list of trade unionists who are either IPA officers or IPA executive committee members.

11 TGWU, *Employee Involvement and Quality Circles – a TGWU Guide*, 1985 edition.

12 F.W.Taylor, *The Principles of Scientific Management*, 1991, Norton edition 1967.

13 Farnham and Pimlott, *op cit*, p65.

14 *Labour Research*, Labour Research Department, August 1989, p8.

15 Marchington, *op cit*, p166.

16 Tom Peters is a well-known and influential management consultant, based in the United States. His philosophy is outlined in Tom Peters and Robert Waterman, *In Search*

of Excellence, Harper and Row, 1982, and Tom Peters' *Thriving on Chaos*, Macmillan, 1988.

17 Union of Communication Workers, Special Branch Circular P32/88, 5.7.88.

18 UCW General Secretary's Annual Report, 1988, pp112-113.

19 Marchington, *op cit*, pp168-9.

20 *Ibid.*

21 For example, the Employment Department Group, *op cit.*

22 *Labour Research*, Labour Research Department, November 1985.

23 There is a useful explanation of these, and other other aspects of quality circles, in Incomes Data Services, *IDS Study 352, Quality Circles*, December 1985, p6.

24 'The "Quality of Life" in GM', International Labour Reports, 1982.

25 *Quality Circles*, TUC, 29.4.81, ref.PB/MC.

26 ACTSS – Administrative, Technical and Supervisory Staffs, the white-collar section of the TGWU.

27 TGWU, *op cit.*

28 *Ibid*, p7.

29 TGWU, *Employee Involvement and Quality Circles*, TGWU policy booklet, 1989 edition.

30 IDS Study 352, *op cit*, p1.

31 Dale and Hayward's survey, University of Manchester Institute of Science and Technology, 1984, results summarised in IDS Study 352, *op cit*, p11.

32 Marchington, *op cit*, p172.

33 Leyland DAF, *News-Link*, special survey issue, February 1989.

34 This tactic was used in autumn 1990 by unions at the Warton site of British Aerospace. See *British Aerospace Warton Unit, Union Opinion Survey*, September 1990, and the survey report, entitled *Working at BAe*, Manchester Employment Research Group Ltd, 1990.

35 This was the role played by the Manchester Employment Research Group in the British Aerospace (Warton) union survey.

36 G.Smith, 'Profit Sharing and Employee Share Ownership in Britain', *Employment Gazette*, August 1986.

37 C. Huhne, 'Lawson unveils profit-related pay plan', *The Guardian*, 16.7.86.

38 Colin Duncan, 'Pay and Payment Systems', in Brian Towers, *op cit*, p235.

39 Source: the US based National Centre for Employee Ownership, as referred to in Terry Dodsworth, 'Millionaires on the shop-floor', *Financial Times*, 6.5.86.

40 'An International Reputation', Unity Trust Bank newsletter, *Unity News*, issue No8, summer 1990, p3.

41 *Ibid.*

42 Duncan, *op cit*, pp244-5.

43 *Ibid*, p245.

44 *Ibid.*

45 The classification suggested by Mick Marchington, *op cit*, pp163-4.

46 Neil Millward, *The New Industrial Relations?*, Policy Studies Institute, 1994.

Chapter 5

Single union agreements – quality initiatives – teamworking

Labour flexibility, just-in-time and employee involvement are fundamental elements of the employers' programme of new management initiatives in the UK since 1979. There are, however, certain other, related new management initiatives which need to be considered to understand recent and current developments in this area of industrial relations.

Single union 'no-strike' deals still only affect a very small percentage of UK workplaces, but the significance of these deals for UK industrial relations is considered greater than their number would suggest. Single union 'no-strike' deals provide the best illustration in the UK to date of how labour flexibility, just-in-time and employee involvement can operate as elements of a fully integrated management programme, which can also protect the vulnerability of just-in-time to industrial action. The more well-known examples, like Nissan, have effectively taken on the role of an industrial relations laboratory for British management, with their influence felt beyond other greenfield sites. This is not to suggest that all is perfect for management under single union deals. Nissan UK, for example, appears to have had serious problems of labour turnover in spite of its location in an area of high unemployment. Single union 'no-strike' deals remain, nevertheless, a challenge to independent trade union organisation in the UK.[1]

Quality initiatives are an increasingly important issue in UK industrial relations. Discussion in previous chapters explained ways in which just-in-time production and employee involvement are related to management initiatives on quality. Current quality initiatives, however, are more complex than this suggests, and are part of a broader development. The relationship between quality improvement and cost saving is an important one, in both private and public sectors. In the public service sector management are promoting new approaches to the quality of service. All the indications are that as money becomes even tighter in the public sector, the application of quality assurance methods will become more prominent.

Teamworking has also been referred to in a previous chapter (on labour flexibility), though its significance is broader than its links with labour flexibility suggest. Teamworking could prove to be one of the most effective vehicles for the introduction of just-in-time, functional flexibility of labour and employee involvement. Its importance appears to lie in its ability to introduce these changes simultaneously and operate an *integrated* approach to their implementation.

Single union deals

Japanese industrial investment in the UK actually began in the early 1970s, but it was not until the 1980s that it commanded serious public attention and became associated with single union agreements. Most, though not all, single union agreements in the UK are with Japanese companies, and most of these are in the motor vehicle and consumer electronics industries. It is not the case, though, that all Japanese companies in the UK operate on the basis of single union deals. And single union deals are not the method used by motor vehicle and electronics companies in Japan. The common method there to achieve similar, but more dramatic ends, is the establishment and operation of company unions. Neither is the single union deal the method used by Japanese multi-nationals in other parts of the world; a common practice of Japanese companies in the USA and elsewhere is to refuse union recognition altogether. (However, there are examples where the United Auto Workers union in the USA has concluded a negotiated settlement with management in joint US-Japanese ventures sufficient to enable a fully-fledged Japanese style management programme to be introduced. These agreements are different again to UK style single union deals.) There are also examples in the UK, including the car industry, of Japanese companies denying union recognition, and using this as the framework for the operation of a fully-fledged programme of new management initiatives and techniques. So it is worth noting that single union deals are *not* some well-tried and tested method of Japanese companies, and their long-term success in managerial terms is uncertain. So why have a number of Japanese companies gone for single union deals in the UK instead of establishing non-union sites? In the case of the 1985 Nissan deal one argument is that the company did have the power to keep the unions out and could have maintained that position for some time, but senior management felt that their energies would have been unnecessarily diverted into fighting off the unions.[2]

It was of course Nissan which really put the single union deal issue on the map, with its site at Washington, near Sunderland. The initial investment was £50 million and the initial workforce 470, but expansion from this starting point has been considerable. A single union agreement was signed by the Amalgamated Union of Engineering Workers in April 1985, and production began in 1986. (At the time the union was known as the AUEW. Its title was changed shortly afterwards to the AEU, and changed yet again in the 1990s to AEEU as a result of its merger with the electricians' union, the EETPU.) The Nissan plant was portrayed as the flagship of new style industrial relations in the climate of Thatcherism. It was evidently perceived by Norman Tebbit, the Trade and Industry Secretary at the time, as a means of provoking change within other motor companies in the UK.[3]

Single union deals and trade union policy

The AUEW's acceptance of the Nissan deal provoked uproar in the trade union movement at the time. The majority of the trade union movement, as expressed through the TUC, were opposed to the way in which such deals were negotiated. It was argued that this resulted in the deal being awarded usually to the union which was prepared to make the most concessions to the new employer, and unions like the TGWU dubbed them 'trade union beauty contests' with the employer as judge. The electricians' union, the EETPU, embraced such methods of negotiation with employers for single

---

Nissan motor manufacturing (UK): facts and figures

By 1988 Nissan was producing 55,000 cars at the Sunderland site. This output figure was to increase four-fold by the early 1990s, reaching 246,000 by 1993, with attention focused on the Micra and Primera. Nissan have taken seriously the aim of maximising local content. The mid-1990s target for the number of EU suppliers represents £450 million of purchased components. In 1994 Nissan had 198 suppliers, two-thirds of which are in the UK. By 1990 production operations at the Sunderland site included pressing, body assembly, painting, plastic injection moulding, engine assembly, engine machining and final assembly. By 1994 the total investment at the site (including government assistance and bank finance) was £900 million, the largest ever single inward investment by a Japanese company in Europe.[4]

The AEU on single union deals

The days of multi-union plants are numbered. The AEU is a singular force among large British unions, promoting and disseminating the sanity of single union agreements.

How can an employer be expected to consult effectively with several unions representing disparate interests?

How can several unions representing disparate interests achieve benefits for the workforce as a whole?

The AEU is and will remain in favour of single union agreements. Companies with whom single union agreements have been negotiated include Iwax (UK) Ltd, NSK Bearings Europe Ltd, Dennis Castings, Dunlop Armaline, Komatsu UK, Servis, Sony (UK) Ltd, Risdon Venesda International Ltd, Coca-Cola and Schweppes, Nissan and many others.[5]

union deals, fully prepared for the competition and conflict with other unions which resulted. This became a direct challenge to the TUC's Bridlington principles, introduced 50 years previously, precisely to discourage inter-union competition and to resolve such disagreements on recruitment and recognition. It was the EETPU's refusal to accept the TUC's decision regarding an inter-union dispute in which the EETPU was involved which led to its eventual expulsion from the TUC, rather than the single union deals issue itself. The apparent choice facing the TUC was either the ultimate expulsion of the EETPU or the repeal of the Bridlington principles. The latter has been fundamental to the way in which the TUC has operated since the 1930s, and therefore it has been argued that the EETPU engineered its own expulsion.

TUC policy and that of most trade unions is opposed to the inter-union rivalry often provoked by the prospect of single union deals on greenfield sites, and the union concessions to employers with which they are associated. Most unions are not opposed to single union agreements *per se*, but they are opposed to single union deals which contain no-strike clauses. The latter has been one of the major concessions made by unions which have been prepared to be a party to Nissan-style deals. The unions which support these agreements argue that they contain no such clauses and are 'strike-free' agreements. This is a point which needs to be clarified.

'No-strike' or 'strike-free' deals?

Those who argue that these agreements are 'strike-free' deals might refer to the particular way in which the agreements are drawn up to support their view. The disputes procedures of such agreements are commonly long-winded and culminate in conciliation and arbitration procedures. The latter may take the form of 'pendulum' arbitration. This means that the arbitration panel will find either entirely for the union's case or entirely for the management's case, and will exclude the possibility of any compromise formula as a basis for settlement. In practice, compromise probably will have taken place, but prior to formal submission to the pendulum arbitration procedure.

However, the reality of a disputes procedure, with lengthy or undefined time periods at some stages, and tied down to conciliation and arbitration in the final stages of the procedure, means that in practice it is very difficult to take industrial action without being 'out of procedure'. As a result, such action is not likely to be made official by the union. Full-time officials are likely to pressurise shop stewards to end the action and management will be confident about suspending and perhaps dismissing workers, and attacking union organisation in such an event.

The argument that these agreements are really 'strike-free' is difficult to justify when such agreements are actually examined. It is also interesting to note that Nissan's president, Takashi Ishihara, advocated a *no-strike deal* rather than a strike-free deal at the time of the Sunderland plant's inauguration. This was in spite of the statements to the press by Nissan UK's personnel director at the time of the agreement with the AUEW, insisting that there was no such thing.[6] It is difficult to avoid the conclusion that the concept of a 'strike-free' deal was little more than a public relations concept used to sell such agreements through the media.

Single union no-strike agreements often contain a range of other ingredients. The no-strike element of the disputes procedure is usually part of a broader management strategy concerned with the relationship between management initiatives on employee involvement, just-in-time production and labour flexibility. The employee involvement and labour flexibility elements are likely to be written into the formal agreement, along with a commitment to teamworking and flexible approaches to training. The just-in-time initiative may or may not be actually written into the agreement. It is, however, often at the very heart of the matter under such single union deals, whether explicitly identified in the agreement or not. A possible explanation for just-in-time agreements being omitted from overall agreements is that management prefer to avoid recognition of any union right to negotiate on just-in-time.

The 'no-strike' clause in the Nissan (UK) agreement

These are the key extracts from the grievance/disputes procedure. Stages 1-3 of the procedure are typical of traditional agreements. The following aspects are not.

'6.a... Stage 4. If the issue is not resolved at Stage 3 it may be referred normally to the Company Council (or a sub-committee thereof) [*the Company Council meets quarterly*] and exceptionally to the Union Divisional Organiser for discussion with appropriate persons nominated by the Company.

b. The company and the Union are totally committed to resolving such matters 'in house' at as early a stage in the procedure as possible. However in exceptional circumstances, if this is not possible, unresolved issues will be referred to the Advisory, Conciliation and Arbitration Service for resolution. This will normally be by conciliation as it is recognised that such issues may not always be appropriate for arbitration. If, however, arbitration is appropriate, the terms of reference will be agreed and the arbitrator will be invited to decide positively in favour of one side or the other.

The arbitrator will be asked to take account of those aspects of the issue which are already agreed. Both parties agree to accept the decision of the arbitrator.

c. In the event of the issue arising from a Company instruction the employee will carry out that instruction pending the completion of the procedure providing the instruction is in accordance with safe working practices.

d. The procedure to Stage 3 must be completed within ten working days of the issue first being raised unless it is mutually agreed at any stage that more time is necessary to ensure that it is resolved at that stage. Following that, the issue will be pursued as expeditiously as possible except that, normally, special meetings of the Company Council will not be arranged.

e. There will be no industrial action of any kind while the issue is in procedure or the subject of conciliation or arbitration.'[7]

Just-in-time, single union deals and industrial action

Just-in-time production is much more vulnerable to industrial action than traditional just-in-case systems of production. There appear to be two *established* ways in which management have resolved this problem:

1. Through destroying independent unions and replacing them with company unions, which is the pattern in certain industries in Japan;

2. Through investment in greenfield and established sites and the denial altogether of union recognition, which is a common approach of Japanese multinationals outside Japan and the UK.

Placed in this context, part of the importance of the no-strike elements of the single union deals in the UK is evident. Just-in-time is particularly important in the highly competitive world markets of the motor industry, and therefore Nissan and Toyota have had to find some means of protection against one of its key weaknesses, that is its vulnerability to industrial action. However, that such companies have also developed very serious programmes of employee involvement is significant in relation to just-in-time's vulnerability. These programmes are intended to play a significant role in creating a workplace culture quite different to those of traditional British workplaces, and to operate in conjunction with the no-strike elements of the procedure in preventing industrial action.

Companies involved in no-strike single union deals also often operate very sophisticated recruitment procedures, with a heavy emphasis on the identification of 'suitable' attitudes of applicants and the use of initial temporary employment contracts or probationary periods for all workers. This is assisted by the fact that most of these companies go for investment in areas of high unemployment. These recruitment policies play an important part in discouraging the employment of trade unionists, and therefore are a further protection against the risk of industrial action under a just-in-time regime.

In turn, it should be remembered that just-in-time production cannot operate without an extensive system of labour flexibility. Workplaces in which single union no-strike deals operate demonstrate very clearly the close relationship between just-in-time, labour flexibility, employee involvement, total quality and teamworking initiatives. A useful way to see these deals is as providing a strong foundation to develop these management initiatives to a greater extent than is normally possible in established union sites.

Quality initiatives

'More and more organisations are emphasising quality in what they do – making steel, filling aerosols, running hotels, looking after peoples' money or looking after their health. Some have adopted a formal system of Total Quality Management; others are seeking to follow their example; and many more are trying to learn the language. Whether it's the pressure of Customer Care programmes in local authorities or international competition in manufacturing, much of the language is the same.'[8]

To clarify the picture it is perhaps helpful to consider the issues under three headings: the reasons for the new emphasis on quality, the management methods, and the implications for trade unions and how they might respond.

Reasons for increased management emphasis on quality

i. *In manufacturing industries,* the introduction of just-in-time production has indeed been important in compelling management and workers to make quality a priority. Just-in-time and quality initiatives often go hand in hand. However, for a variety of reasons just-in-time may not be feasible for certain manufacturing companies. For example, the technology essential for their particular industry may make short production runs with rapid and frequent change-overs and re-setting of machinery, equipment or plant out of the question. This does not mean that total quality initiatives are unlikely to be a key issue in the absence of just-in-time. *Achieving the twin goals of a lower price and better quality of design and manufacture is still central to the task of winning customers in the climate of intensified competition.*

The combination of national and international factors have created a much more intense battle for market share, rather than a battle for new markets, for many companies in most sectors of manufacturing. This inten- sification of competition has brought about a search for new manufacturing and management methods, either to overtake competitors or simply to remain in the market. Whether it is quality initiatives in conjunction with just-in-time or without it, management motivation for the initiatives is essentially the same.

However, to divorce the question of quality improvement from the question of cost reduction in this context of intensified competition would be naive. Emphasis on quality may mean a genuine improvement in the quality of design and manufacture, but it may mean simply a change to a cheaper method of quality control through the replacement of inspection functions by 'right first time' methods, and production workers stamping their own work. In the case of the latter, the reality may be a crude cost- cutting exercise in the guise of managerial commitment to improving quality. This will reap only short-term gains over competitors, and management will probably be forced to return to the question of genuine improvement in the quality of design and manufacture. But obviously this too incorporates cost reduction. As one well-known manufacturer put it, the 'right first time' approach adopted by everyone in the workplace can save millions, and therefore the key is to become proficient at *preventing* problems, rather than to excel at resolving them.[9] If quality means reduction in costs, this may also make a contribution towards maintaining a competitive price for the products sold in the market. In fact many companies are focusing on the concept of value to the customer as a means of integrating their quality and price strategies.

ii. *The public sector* too is experiencing important management initiatives on quality. These are portrayed as aiming to improve the service to the user, referred to as the 'customer' or 'client', and are evident, for example, in the National Health Service, postal services, passenger transport services, post-16 education and local authority services including housing, refuse collection, schools and social services. So what are the management motives for these initiatives?

Management in all parts of the public sector are now significantly influenced by private enterprise culture, with the adoption of many of the ideas and concepts of private industry. Whilst some public sector managers may lack a clear understanding of the developments in labour flexibility, just-in-time, employee involvement, teamworking and single union deal issues in private industry, they are particularly conscious of and increasingly accountable to market forces. This can be largely explained in terms of three closely related aspects of government policy:

    a. privatisation and the threat of it;

    b. the on-going programme of public spending cuts;

    c. financial delegation and the dismantling of public sector organisations.

The relationship between spending cuts, value for money and quality initiatives in the public sector is an important one. Public sector management are increasingly desperate to provide the best possible service, *whatever that may be*, for the least possible cost. When put in this context it becomes evident that quality can be seen in terms of efficiency and effectiveness.

However, the issue may also have another dimension. Whilst Labour and Liberal Democrat local authorities have felt free to pass on the blame for cuts to Conservative governments, Conservative councils and particularly Conservative governments have been faced with the problem of carrying out sometimes very extensive cuts and at the same time needing to argue that this is in the public interest. They have tried to argue that through improvements in efficiency and effectiveness, the service is being improved. Therefore, governments faced with such dilemmas may have a political interest in encouraging public sector management initiatives on quality of service to users, not only because of the efficiency aspect, but also because of their possible concern about the response of public opinion to cuts in public services.[10]

Another factor is the influence which just-in-time philosophy may be having on public sector management thinking. Such ideas can be applied to non-manufacturing sectors, and it is possible that they have a bearing on the public sector debate about quality.

Management methods and tools for improving quality

There are a wide range of methods at the disposal of private sector management to deal with quality concerns. Public sector management has only more recently become aware of some of these methods, and it would seem that many sections of public sector management have focused on the quality methods which the private sector were experimenting with some years ago, and have yet to learn some of the more recent lessons of the private sector. However, experience in the private sector is by no means evenly spread.

i. *British Standard 5750* has become an issue in relation to quality in both private industry and the public sector. BS 5750 is equivalent to the international standard ISO 9000 and European standard EN 29000. Employers applying for BS 5750 will be assessed, and if awarded the standard are likely to publicise the fact to their customers and potential customers. The related standard ISO 9001 is also significant in industry. The Ministry of Defence operate AQAP (Allied Quality Assurance Publication) standards for the large number of companies which carry out contract work for it. In 1991 BS 5750 was extended with specific provision for service industries (BS 5750 Part 8) and software companies (BS 5750 Part 13). To attain BS 5750 the company or public sector organisation in question has to demonstrate that it has established an effective quality assurance system, whether within a defined section of the organisation or the organisation as a whole, to ensure that its own specifications of quality of product or service are met. It is perhaps significant that BS 5750 does not in itself assess the definition of acceptable quality drawn up by the company or public sector organisation, but rather whether the company's quality assurance system is adequate to meet it. It is reasonable to conclude from this that BS 5750 is inadequate in itself and only a piece in the total quality jigsaw. Management critics of BS 5750 have complained that the accreditation process is unduly bureaucratic. In spite of this 20,000 organisations had applied for BS 5750/ISO

9000 registration by 1993, more than the whole of the rest of Europe put together.[11]

ii. *Statistical process control, the 'seven tools' and 'poka-yoke'* refer to a combined approach to total quality control. Statistical process control (SPC), or statistical quality control as it is sometimes known, is quite a common quality control tool used in UK manufacturing, and is not a new idea.[12] Essentially it involves the sampling of key measurements and analysing their variation from exact specification through the use of graphs and percentages, in order to identify problem areas and improve quality. Some managers in UK manufacturing may see SPC as the Japanese answer to many of their quality control problems. However, there is evidence to suggest that companies in Japan (at least in the car industry) adopt a slightly different approach. This was the lesson learnt by Nissan (UK)'s plant quality manager, Arthur David, on a visit to sister sites in Japan.[13] He assumed he would find the liberal use of SPC methods at those sites, but was surprised to find instead the use of a range of methods to ensure quality (including SPC), and with a strong emphasis on employee involvement throughout. The focus of attention was kept on the practical task of improving quality, with a flexible use of different quality control techniques as required. The Japanese refer to these as the 'seven tools'. SPC is one of these; *poka-yoke* is another.

Poka-yoke is a technique which entails the design of production processes which do not allow faults to be made by operatives. *Poka-yoke* can be translated as 'careless mistake proofing' or 'fool-proofing'. It is seen at Nissan sites in Japan, and presumably at Nissan (UK) as well now, as an important technique in the drive for zero defects.

Nissan's view of the 'seven tools' of quality control

The UK approach to quality control in the car industry has been to focus attention on statistical process control. The approach in car plants in Japan is to use what is effectively a toolbox of seven quality control techniques. The toolbox includes SPC, but also *poka-yoke*, fish-bone design analysis, FMEA, and other techniques. The principle of a conventional toolbox is employed in the sense that Japanese car plant workers select the appropriate quality technique for the particular problem, and therefore all car workers are normally trained in all seven techniques. In this way product quality, continuous improvement and customer satisfaction are never lost sight of.[14]

---

iii. *Total quality management* or TQM is a concept which rejects the traditional notion of leaving the responsibility for quality to a specialist group of inspectors. However, it is much more than this. At Nissan (UK), for example, TQM means that quality is the responsibility of every single employee, that it runs through every part of the business, and that there are particular ways in which every employee can contribute to continuously improving quality at the plant.[15]

One of the problems with TQM is that the term has been used in industrial relations circles in rather confusing ways. Some uses of the term have referred narrowly to the operation of BS5750 alongside statistical process control and their implementation throughout the workplace. This might be referred to as the 'conformance to specifications' approach. Other definitions have seen initiatives to change employees' attitudes and the involvement and increased commitment of people in the workplace as central to their TQM programme. Yet other TQM concepts go further, adopting the conformity to specifications approach and the emphasis on people in the organisation, but also integrating the programme with supplier networks, internal customers and external customers, and emphasising precisely what customers want in terms of quality. A fourth level of TQM development incorporates all this, but focuses on continuously improving *value to the customer*, an approach which addresses the question of price as well as genuine customer requirements on quality. Nicholls has made sense of the confusion about the meaning of TQM by identifying these four phases and seeing TQM as an evolutionary process.[16] It would appear that his perspective is not yet widely shared by management in the UK. Nicholls also argues that organisations which attempt to jump in at phase three of four of the TQM process are more likely to fail than if they had worked through the TQM process phase by phase.

Where TQM is implemented alongside just-in-time production methods, a broader concept is likely to emerge for several reasons. *Kaizen* (continuous improvement) philosophy and teamworking techniques are important ingredients in effective JIT programmes, but they can also play a significant part in broadening out management's approach to TQM (which itself is an essential ingredient in an effective JIT programme). In addition, JIT makes all weaknesses and faults in the production system conspicuous and therefore it is difficult for management and workers alike to avoid finding effective and lasting solutions to them. This makes a well-developed and effective total quality programme essential. Management confusion about TQM concepts and the adoption of narrower definitions is more likely to arise in workplaces where just-in-time is not on the agenda.

In some workplaces, management announce that an alternative route to TQM has been adopted. When examined more closely most of these programmes reside somewhere within the broad four phase TQM framework suggested by Nicholls. The problem arises from the narrow interpretation of the TQM concept. However, it should be said that Nicholls does recognise that the fourth, most developed phase of TQM is close to transcending the notion of *quality* with its concept of *value* to the customer.

There are also examples where TQM has been linked to the TECs' Investors in People initiative. Whilst the TECs' Investors in People initiative emphasises training and human resource management, central to its approach is the use of standards not dissimilar to performance indicators, which are evidently influenced by the Citizen's Charter concept.

iv. *Quality circles* (see the chapter on employee involvement) were first used by British companies in about 1978. There were many early failures of this method, but there have been more recent successes, with management sometimes introducing quality circles under a different name. They have come to be concerned with many issues in addition to quality, and could now be more accurately referred to as problem-solving groups.

v. *Teamworking*, whilst not a quality technique in itself, can play a particularly important part in creating a group culture which leads to significant improvements in quality. Essentially, teamworking can create a situation in which team members become dependent on each other to maintain key aspects of their working conditions. The intention is to set teams and their tasks up in such a way that mistakes and lack of effort have repercussions for other team members. The group pressure which results can play a very effective part, in conjunction with JIT and *kaizen*, in finding permanent solutions to quality problems. Of course, the implications for the workforce raise other questions.

Quality initiatives: implications and the trade union response

It is not easy for trade unions to question management campaigns and initiatives to improve the quality of their products or services. However, there are some opportunities for unions to do so.

In the case of manufacturing, the argument in defence of quality initiatives by management is that improved quality combined with lower prices are the ingredients for survival in increasingly competitive markets. This argument is likely to carry some weight with employees, especially when supported with fear of redundancy.

Detrimental effects for employees include job losses and/or redeployment which will result from the transfer of quality control responsibilities from inspectors to production workers. These kinds of initiatives mean changes in working practices (an extension of functional flexibility) for production workers, and indicate new training and re-training requirements. Those companies which advocate total quality management are suggesting the application of this principle throughout the factory. Increased workloads may well result, but may not be reflected in workers' wage packets. Trade unions will gain if they can get information about management's cost savings which result from such initiatives, since they will be able to make use of it in negotiation. It is possible that management may be willing to release these figures, since they are their prime measure of the success of a quality campaign, and they may well choose to publicise these figures as part of their employee involvement strategy to change workplace attitudes.

Quality initiatives in the public service sector take on a slightly different complexion. Public sector unions have campaigned long and hard against cuts in public spending, suggesting that cuts mean a reduced quality of service. The current quality initiatives of management in public services are an attempt to challenge this connection. They have borrowed the idea from the private sector of improving quality and reducing cost simultaneously. This presents a difficult challenge to the established policy of public service unions. They may be tempted to quietly ignore these quality initiatives because of an inhibition to challenge any initiatives which may be perceived as improving the service to the public.

If no significant response explicitly directed at the quality initiatives of management is forthcoming from public sector unions, then the application of these initiatives to public services may result in job loss and/or redeployment, increased functional flexibility, increased workloads without compensation in wages, and new training and re-training initiatives, that is, consequences not dissimilar to those for manufacturing. The implementation of total quality initiatives in public services may also help to legitimise the politically-loaded argument that cuts do not necessarily mean a deterioration in the quality of service, which in turn may pave the way for further rounds of cuts.

If many public sector workers are badly paid, suffer poor conditions and lack job security, and quality initiatives are introduced which make this even worse, then they may not have the stamina to guarantee the high standard of service which the public demands. If the general levels of morale amongst most types of public service workers are particularly low, this may prove to be a fundamental obstacle to the genuine improvement of the quality of service, regardless of management efforts. The implications of total quality initiatives may mean further cost-cutting and increased demands and stress for these workers, which will probably bring about a further decline in morale. In the case of the 'caring professions', such as nurses, social workers and teachers, a sense of personal commitment has been and continues to be essential for the provision of high quality services in these occupations. Poor pay, excessive workloads and bad conditions, declining job security, and the prospect of further deterioration in these as a result of *private enterprise-style* quality initiatives, will probably have several results. It may increase the numbers of highly trained staff determined to leave these jobs at the first opportunity, which will encourage skill shortages. It is likely to contribute to serious problems of occupational ill-health in these occupations (particularly stress-related illnesses). It will encourage such workers to abandon their sense of commitment to the job, feeling incapable of influencing the situation, and thus contribute to a deterioration in the quality of service rather than its improvement. In spite of the trends of the 1980s and early 1990s, a feasible outcome could be assertive expressions of industrial action.

Public sector unions stand to gain if they can establish any of the following conditions for the introduction of total quality programmes in particular workplaces.

a. No job loss as a result.

b. Any redeployment to be negotiated and not to result in loss of pay.

c. Any increase in functional flexibility to be clearly defined and not to amount to a deterioration of conditions.

d. No increase in workloads regardless of financial incentives, in light of the health implications and the already seriously over-stretched situation of employees in respect of their working conditions.

e. Where training/retraining results from management's initiatives on quality, then opportunities might be opened up for training which would be recognised by other employers, and which would genuinely improve the prospects of those workers who participate in it, rather than simply solving a short-term management problem.

Teamworking

Teamworking raises issues much wider than its common association with labour flexibility, important as this is. Incomes Data Services suggested in

1988 that UK management interest in teamworking was significantly increasing, and there are good reasons to expect UK management to pay further attention to teamworking in the 1990s.

It may be helpful to clarify some of the terms in use. The idea of working as a team is at the heart of employee involvement philosophy. It implies that conflict in industrial relations is not inevitable, that harmony between management and workers is possible, and that it is in the interests of all to operate as one large team if success is to be achieved in the competition with the 'teams' of other companies. This is a unitary perspective of industrial relations.[17] Used in this sense the team idea refers to a unity of interest throughout one particular workplace or company.

Often, however, the team idea is used more specifically. The idea of establishing and building teams may be used to refer to a particular approach to management organisation. With essentially the same underlying philosophy, it is commonly used to refer to small groups of workers numbering between five and twenty who carry out shopfloor tasks as teams. It is this meaning to which the terms teamworking, the team concept, group working and autonomous work groups refer.

Teamworking in practice: the IBC (Luton) agreement

In the earlier chapter on labour flexibility, an agreement at IBC (Luton) (the former Bedford van plant) was referred to, illustrating the relationship between teamworking and labour flexibility. A study of the rest of the team concept section of this agreement is instructive. It illustrates the connection between teamworking and the full range of new management initiatives, and explains clearly the essential ingredients of teamworking. These are as follows:

    a. team responsibility for quality improvement;

    b. team responsibility for on-going cost saving exercises;

    c. employee involvement and the encouragement of team attitudes;

    d. full functional flexibility within the team;

    e. application of the principle of 'continuous improvement' (or *kaizen*);

    f. the take-over of certain managerial responsibilities previously allocated to supervisors;

    g. team responsibility for training for all tasks within the team.

In fact, the IBC agreement includes one or two further elements in addition to this list.

The IBC (Luton) agreement on teamworking, 1987

A. The Team Concept.

i. The team concept is a critical part of the new manufacturing system that will allow the company to be a producer of world class quality products at a competitive cost thereby contributing to the long term viability of the company and long term job security for its employees.

ii. The key ingredient is the concept that employees have an opportunity to impact the success of the business through decision making, pride in their work and cooperative efforts among each other.

iii. This process requires joint participation, mutual trust, respect and recognises employees as the most important investment and resource.

iv. The functional catalyst of the team concept, therefore, are the team members and the team leaders who share responsibilities.

v. Team members share the responsibility for:

1. work performed by the team.

2. rotating jobs within the team.

3. ensuring quality of team output.

4. maintaining a safe, clean and tidy work area.

5. continually striving for improvement in operations cost, quality and productivity, e.g., scrap and waste reduction, keeping quality and maintenance records, etc.

6. establishing and achieving team goals.

7. acquiring job knowledge to fulfil all jobs within the team.

8. being a self sufficient team by performing duties previously performed by other disciplines, e.g. self-inspection, repair, minor maintenance.

9. maintain regular attendance – all share and cover the work of absent colleagues.

vi The team involves employees working together as a functional group in the overall manufacture and assembly of a vehicle.[18]

The American experience of teamworking

Some informative work on the subject of teamworking and the team concept has been carried out by trade union researchers in the USA, particularly Jane Slaughter and the team who work for *Labor Notes*.[19] In a recent article, Slaughter draws attention to the relationship between Taylorism and teamworking, and the role of teamworking in intensifying the pace of work.[20] The important point that Slaughter makes is that in effect teamworking asks workers to carry out time-and-motion studies on themselves. She argues that rather than having been discarded, Taylorism is reasserting itself through teamworking.

Slaughter's reports on developments in the United States emphasise the importance of the team concept and teamworking as an essential vehicle for the simultaneous introduction of the management initiatives associated with just-in-time, employee involvement, labour flexibility, total quality and continuous improvement. Her reports centre on such developments at the several joint American-Japanese car plants in the USA, notable of which is the Toyota-General Motors NUMMI site (New United Motors Manufacturing Inc plant) at Fremont, California.

NUMMI is the model for how work in many industries might be organised in the near future, not only in the motor vehicle industry, where it is already well-advanced, but in many others including the steel, electrical, paper and telephone industries, which are already exploring the team concept. US management journals refer to the system as 'synchronous manufacturing' although 'management by stress' would be a better name.[21]

It would appear that this plant has had a similar (if not greater) impact on US industrial relations to that of Nissan on UK industrial relations. Important differences are that NUMMI was not greenfield, but an old factory, with a unionised workforce and low investment in new technology. There are some interesting parallels here with the Rover-Honda agreement in the UK. Changes in management methods and industrial relations were radical. The result at NUMMI has been the production of cars which evidently do compete with Japanese imports. Teamworking has been right at the heart of the NUMMI venture.

Teamworking: implications and the trade union response
Teamworking has great potential as a management tool for the implementation of new management initiatives and techniques programmes. There has to be doubt about whether unions in the UK have attached a sufficient degree of importance to teamworking. Unions may be significantly disadvantaged if they fail to treat teamworking as a key issue in negotiations about new management initiatives. Teamworking is central to most single union 'no-strike' agreements, but most unions in private industry face the issue in the context of negotiation on functional labour flexibility. Unions may find negotiations on a pay rise or a reduction in the working week linked to functional flexibility, and that some kind of agreement in principle on the phased introduction of teamworking may be appended to this. An effective trade union response to teamworking depends significantly on the

combination of union policy objectives in relation to the functional flexibility of labour, just-in-time, employee involvement techniques, total quality initiatives and continuous improvement.

However, teamworking does have its weaknesses. One of them is that teamworking is a vehicle for just-in-time, and a key weakness of just-in-time is its vulnerability to industrial action. Another problem for many sections of British management in the introduction of employee involvement is the difficulty it faces in establishing a new workplace culture because of the contradiction between coercive and conciliatory styles of management. Teamworking is an important vehicle for the introduction of employee involvement, and therefore union exploitation of this problem of contradictory management styles will not only inhibit the development of employee involvement, but also restrict the full potential for management of teamworking. Another possible weakness of teamworking is related to the speed at which functional flexibility of labour is introduced. In unionised workplaces, in the late 1980s at least, UK management had been forced generally to adopt a more gradual approach to the introduction of functional flexibility than was the case in the early and mid-1980s. If this slow speed of change is maintained in the 1990s, this too will act as a brake on UK management's realisation of the full potential of teamworking.

Based on the American experience of teamworking and the team concept, Jane Slaughter draws attention to three further important points.[22] First, as with single union 'no-strike' deals in the UK, employers could not have easily introduced their 'blockbuster' team concept/teamworking agreements in the US car industry without major concessions and a basic shift in policy made by key sections of the union (the United Auto Workers). However, the UAW rank and file have started to react to this by organising opposition groups and caucuses within the union. At sites where the team concept has been introduced, these groups have begun to win union positions, displacing those local union leaders who welcomed the new management methods. A respectable number of union positions have even been won at the model NUMMI General Motors-Toyota site by such an opposition group within the union. Such initiatives are a reflection of a minority radical and left-wing tradition of the US labour movement.

The second point is concerned with the diffusion of the team concept and teamworking methods, and the just-in-time, labour flexibility, employee involvement, total quality and continuous improvement dimensions associated with it. It is concerned with the momentum of intensified competition which drives management to introduce these methods. The logic of this process, which typifies the economic development of capitalism to a stage even beyond the control of multinationals, is that any business advantage gained over competitors through the introduction of the new management methods may be only temporary, until competitors in turn adopt similar methods. Furthermore, as Slaughter points out, however much the new methods increase the pace of work, there are those elsewhere who will do the same, and for less pay. The similarities between this process and the diffusion of just-in-case and early assembly line methods following their introduction by Ford some eighty years ago are enlightening. The way in which the Ford assembly line methods spread first through the car industry, and then to other industries is essentially the same as the process we are witnessing today, even though the management methods are different. This is particularly well illustrated by Braverman's account of the diffusion of Ford's assembly line methods.[23]

A final point drawn from Slaughter's articles emphasises the importance of increasingly stressful working conditions as opposed to pay as the potential key motivator in a union response to teamworking. In 1930s America non-union car workers reached the point when they would take no more, occupied their factories and joined the union, the UAW. The circumstances which provoked this response were not wage issues but arbitrary management and the exhausting pace of work. Slaughter suggests that the parallels with teamworking are evident in light of the 'management by stress' principle which is an essential ingredient of a *fully developed* team concept and teamworking programme. In such working environments the sentiments of union and non-union labour may focus primarily on this particular aspect of teamworking. Or as an unknown American auto worker of the 1930s put it, 'I ain't got no kick on wages. I just don't like to be drove.'[24]

Notes

1   However, the Policy Studies Institute research does cast doubt on just how significant single union no-strike deals have been in the UK during the mid 1980s to early 1990s period: Neil Millward, *The New Industrial Relations?*, Policy Studies Institute, 1994.
2   Peter Hetherington, 'Nissan union deal "an example for BL"', *The Guardian*, 23.4.85.
3   Hetherington, *op cit.*
4   Brendan Coyne, 'Nissan – continually improving quality', *Quality Today*, March 1989, p33; Andrew Lorenz, 'The British Car is Dead', *Management Today*, August 1994.
5   Amalgamated Engineering Union, *Creating the Union of the Future*, document issued by the union's Executive Council, 1988.
6   John Ardill, 'Single union at Nissan UK plant', *The Guardian*, 23.4.85.
7   Nissan Motor Manufacturing (UK) Limited, *Agreement and Conditions of Employment*, 1.1.87, extracts from para. 6, 'Procedure'.

8   *Measuring Efficiency*, Incomes Data Services, Focus No57, December 1990, p7.

9   *Leyland Engines Newsletter*, Issue 15, February 1986.

10 See, for example, *The Health Service – The NHS Reforms and You*, Department of Health, July 1990.

11 *Quality in Practice: BS5750 and Kaizen*, BBC publicity to accompany training video of the same name, 1993.

12 The idea of statistical process control was first proposed by Walter A. Shewhart in *Economic Control of Manufactured Products*, 1931. In the same book he drew attention to the relationship between improving quality and reducing costs.

13 Coyne, *op cit.*

14 *Ibid*, pp33-4.

15 *Ibid*, p34.

16 John Nicholls, 'TQM's direction shifts paradigms', *Management Consultancy*, May 1993, pp53-61.

17 This is in contrast to pluralist perspectives of industrial relations which portray unions and employers as 'competing interest groups', and also to Marxist perspectives which see conflict, in one form or another, as central to and inevitable in, the relationship between labour and capital.

18 *Flexible Working*, Incomes Data Services, Study No407, April 1988, p19.

19 See J. Slaughter, 'Teaming Up – Against the Union', *International Labour Reports*, No27-28, Summer 1988, pp9-10; J. Slaughter, 'Sparks fly on the factory floor', *New Internationalist*, May 1989, pp24-5; J. Slaughter (co-author), 'Choosing Sides: Unions and the Team Concept', *Labor Notes*, 1988 (available from *Labor Notes*, 7435 Michigan Avenue, Detroit, MI48210, USA, tel.313-842-6262).

20 Slaughter, 'Sparks', *op cit.*

21 *Ibid.*

22 Slaughter, 'Teaming Up', *op cit*; Slaughter, 'Sparks', *op cit.*

23 Harry Braverman, *Labor and Monopoly Capital*, Monthly Review Press, 1974, pp146-51.

24 Slaughter, 'Teaming Up', *op cit.*

Chapter 6

New management initiatives – the future in the UK

This chapter is divided into four areas of interest regarding the possible future development of the new management initiatives in the UK. It considers the possible impact of the changes in Europe, the implications of recession, the future direction of Conservative government policy and the alternative policies of the Labour Party and the Liberal Democrats.

New management initiatives and changes in Europe

In the 1990s Europe is going through a more rapid and complex period of change, with a greater degree of economic and political instability, than at any time since the aftermath of the Second World War. Dramatic, unpredictable and disturbing as developments are in Eastern Europe, this is also an accurate description of the European Union states. Inseparably linked to the future of the EU is the question of industrial and commercial rationalisation and the intensification of competition. International trade relationships between EU and non-EU states and companies also raise questions of intensification of competition. There are the immense difficulties of identifying and exploiting new markets in Eastern Europe and the former Soviet Union. All these questions relate to battles for market share as opposed to the prospects of finding new markets, and this in turn is directly connected with the speed and extent of the growth of new management techniques.

The European Union (EU) – known in earlier years as the EC, EEC or the Common Market – has had a chequered history. Established under the Treaty of Rome in 1957, it was initially composed of six countries – France, West Germany, Italy, Belgium, the Netherlands and Luxembourg. By the early 1990s it was made up of twelve, the six new additions being the UK, Denmark, Ireland, Portugal, Spain and Greece. At the time of writing, four more countries were in the process of joining, bringing the total to sixteen. There are also added complications as a result of the fundamental political changes in Eastern Europe, not least in relation to German reunification and the consequences of this for the German economy (prior to reunification the strongest of the 'twelve'), and for the EU as a whole. In July 1987 the Single European Act came into force. In general terms this committed the EU member states to achieve a *single European market*, in which there would be *free movement of goods, services, capital and labour* between all EU countries through the removal of obstacles to competition. Its economic, monetary, political and social implications are immense.

The Single European Act set in motion a series of events which are central to the process of economic, monetary and political union of the EU states. In particular the Conservative government in the UK took a hard line in opposition both to proposals for a single European currency and for the Social Chapter. This government position was reflected in the Maastricht summit in 1991 and the resultant Treaty on European Union. The agreement at Maastricht gave the UK exemption on both these issues. Exemption from the Social Chapter of the Treaty has important implications for the implementation of new management initiatives in the UK.

Economic integration and the European Union

With an EU population of 324 million, a single European market for the Union offers the promise to big business of creating a trading bloc of greater significance than any other world-wide. Of course, whether the promise will be realised remains to be seen. The Cecchini Report, produced for the European Commission in 1986, outlined the economic rationale behind the Single European Market.[1] It drew attention to the increased competition and extensive economies arising from the reorganisation of business as larger scale operations. Cecchini suggested that costs would be cut as a result, and that this in turn would bring about a fall in prices; demand would be thus stimulated, leading to economic growth, further restructuring, and innovation and technical progress. Others have put a slightly different interpretation upon the Single European Market's implications of increased competition and the economies of larger scale production.

European big business interests '…are conscious that, for example, in the EC there are 300 firms making domestic appliances, whilst in the USA there are only four. There are 13 locomotive builders compared with two in the US.

The European capitalists hope that the free movement of labour and goods will enable them to rationalise their operations, force out less efficient firms and intensify the exploitation of the working class. Through mergers and buy-outs they hope to create giant monopolies which can compete with the American and Japanese combines on the world market.'[2]

Clearly, the specific implications for employers will vary, depending upon the size and structure of their company, their current geographical locations and the characteristics of the product markets in which they operate.

i. Export opportunities within the EU for UK-based companies will generally increase (notwithstanding other factors such as recession), but so will the opportunities for companies based in other EU countries to export to the UK. Competition will thus intensify and the trend will be towards increasingly large scale production to meet larger markets.

ii. Whilst *some* medium-sized and small companies *may* be unaffected because of localised or specialised markets, those medium-sized and small companies which operate in similar product markets to multinationals are at risk of being taken-over or going out of business.

iii. The intensification of competition *between multinationals* within the EU will continue, with many more large-scale mergers and take-overs.

iv. If national obstacles to competition are increasingly removed, several factors are likely to be more prominent in influencing the investment decisions of multinationals. These include variations in labour costs, in the availability of skilled labour, in transport facilities and geographical location. Where multinationals are already located in areas with disadvantages in terms of location and transport facilities, then pressures upon them will probably increase either to move their investment elsewhere or to find ways of reducing labour costs to compensate.

v. An *increase* in the geographical imbalance in terms of investment and economic development is a serious possibility.

vi. Companies located outside the EU (or with inadequate location within it) have already shown their desperation not to be excluded from 'Fortress Europe' either through attempts to take over EU companies (eg, Nestle's take-over of Rowntree) or to establish large-scale sites within the EU prior to 1992 (eg, Nissan, Honda and Toyota in the UK).

Before considering the possible effects of intensification of competition on the new management initiatives, it is perhaps helpful to distinguish between *the search for new product markets, and battles for market share*. The search for new markets sounds simple when posed as a question of a company identifying new groups of people with the necessary purchasing power and the willingness to buy the product. This can be done through a variety of means – including advertising, credit facilities, the reduction of prices, improvements in the product. Battles for market share, on the other hand, emphasise the strategy and tactics adopted by companies to win over customers from their competitors. Wherever possible companies are likely to attempt to identify a niche in the market for their products in order to minimise the threat from competitors, if only to gain a temporary competitive advantage. The reality for most companies is that they are forced to be involved in both the search for new markets and battles for market share, but the extent to which the emphasis is on one of these rather than the other will vary according to the characteristics of that particular product market.

In light of the massive productive capacity of the multinational companies, there is a desperation on their part to identify and exploit new markets. The extent to which they fail to do this will dictate the intensity of battles for market share and emphasise a crisis of overproduction. These questions are highly relevant, not only to the situation within the EU, but also to the question of potential for new markets in Eastern Europe and the former Soviet Union.

The considerable intensification of competition brought about by the prospect of the Single European Market and greater economic integration within the EU is forcing companies to establish more competitive pricing policies, to ensure better quality in design and manufacture of their product, faster delivery and a better after-sales service to the customer. All these factors are particularly emphasised in battles for market share, and it would not be unreasonable to expect this battle to be the predominant concern of multinationals in respect of markets within the EU.

EU economic integration and just-in-time, labour flexibility and total quality initiatives

In light of the factors discussed above, it would not be surprising if increasing economic integration within the EU is an important factor in encouraging a much more widespread introduction of just-in-time in both manufacturing and non-manufacturing sectors, since JIT provides the potential to cut costs by reduction in the proportion of capital tied down in the production (or work) process, to improve quality and provide a better customer service. Greater economic integration of the EU is likely to encourage new management initiatives across the continent – whether they are introduced in conjunction with JIT or not – particularly initiatives by multinationals which aim to bring about a substantially greater degree of functional and temporal flexibility of labour. Increasing economic integration for the EU is also likely to be an important factor in encouraging total quality initiatives – whether related to JIT or not – in both private and public sectors.

The Social Chapter: implications for labour flexibility and employee involvement

The fact that the Treaty on European Union (Maastricht) has given the British government exemption from the Social Chapter of that treaty has the effect of encouraging the growth of numerical flexibility of labour in the UK. However, in spite of the Social Chapter 'opt out', the Conservatives' commitment to numerical flexibility may face an increasing challenge through the courts. Numerical flexibility refers to the use by employers of part-time, temporary and casual labour (see chapter three). The adoption of the Social Chapter by the other eleven EU states will probably discourage the worst examples of exploitation of such labour, and probably generally discourage EU employers outside the UK from making numerical flexibility of labour an important ingredient in their implementation of new management techniques.

The Social Chapter means that the right of member states to exercise a veto over European Union decisions no longer applies to certain employment issues. Instead a system of qualified majority voting applies (a system which gives countries votes according to their size). The Social Chapter extends qualified majority voting from health and safety issues to information and consultation of employees, working conditions, sex equality in employment and integration of workers excluded from the labour market. However, European Union member states still have to vote unanimously regarding decisions on social security directives, redundancy rights and conditions of employment for third country nationals.[3]

UK exemption from the Social Chapter may also have the effect of encouraging many employers in this country to continue to follow a particularly British route in respect of employee involvement. Conservative government policy has advocated consistently, with support from British employers, a voluntary approach to employee involvement. It has been quite unsympathetic to employee participation concepts, which represent the predominant approach within the EU. Directives resulting from the Social Chapter may well strengthen EU concepts of employee participation by, for example, extending workers' rights to company information in the event of redundancies, take-overs and changes in working practices. Conversely, exemption from the Social Chapter may encourage many employers in the UK not only to rigidly restrict employee involvement to an emphasis on consultation, but also to concede little in respect of the range of information employees are to be consulted about. However, the situation faced by multinationals with large sites in both the UK and other EU states will be more complex than this.

EU economic integration: effects on trade union power, challenges to trade union independence and employee involvement

Increasing economic integration in Western Europe may bring about a number of developments which will discourage industrial action by trade unions.

Trade union power across the EU is likely to face a major challenge in terms of *unemployment*. The Cecchini Report itself suggested job losses would be around 0.5 million in 1993 alone as a result of the abolition of customs posts, transit agents, etc.[4] The changes to taxation could bring further substantial job losses. Perhaps most serious of all, however, are the restrictions on state aid to private companies to encourage free competition, and the restructuring of both industrial and service sectors which is likely to take place on a massive scale. John Harvey-Jones has suggested that over a ten year period we will witness the closure of half of Europe's factories and half of its companies will disappear or be absorbed by mergers.[5]

In the course of industrial rationalisation, it would be no surprise if trade unions across the European Union faced increasingly bitter confrontations with multinationals. If unions attempt, increasingly, to reorganise on a European scale in response to such rationalisation, the emergence of increasing tensions and conflicts within unions is a serious possibility. What kind of trade union policy might start to emerge at a European level in the different industrial sectors? Might it be a European version of 'new

---

The way capital will develop, post 1992?

The restructuring of the British economy of the past decade put millions out of work, created a North/South divide and a contracting and deteriorating public sector. The British experience could provide a model for the way capital will develop in Europe post-1992.[6]

---

realism', or even the promotion of a new 'corporatism'? This is an important question in relation to the development of new management initiatives, since it is feasible that a trade union leadership could emerge on a European scale which might usher in initiatives associated with just-in-time, total quality management, employee involvement and labour flexibility. Multinationals may go increasingly, for example, for 'block-buster' labour flexibility deals linked to high wage agreements. There is one particular area, however, which may cause serious difficulty for trade union independence in the 1990s and that is employee involvement.

As stated previously, *employee involvement* can have an important role to play in assisting the introduction of the new management techniques. Many would argue that employee involvement and participation are taken more seriously in most other European countries than they are in the UK. The British government's position has been to insist on the merits of a voluntary approach in which there is no legal requirement on companies to introduce employee involvement or participation systems. Whilst systems vary in the EU, the absence of any statutory basis in the UK (other than the very limited provision of the 1982 Employment Act) is largely the exception amongst EU countries. Works councils and workplace committees of a variety of different kinds can be set up under the law in most other EU countries. Some are joint employer-employee committees, others are employee-only committees, and there is a difference between those countries which give priority to trade union candidates for such committees and those which make no distinction between union and non-union candidates. There is provision in law in some countries for works council representation on company boards.[7] This situation means some uncertainty in terms of how employee involvement issues will develop in the 1990s. It is further complicated by the prospects of a new EU directive which addresses these and related issues.

One interpretation of the Conservative governments' opposition to any imposed system of employee involvement is that they are concerned that some EU countries place more emphasis on participation than involvement, and that a situation might develop in the UK in which management might be unable to maintain the initiative on the issue as they have been able to do to date. When the emphasis is on participation, it can turn out to be a slippery slope for management as well as trade unions.

Quite how Conservative government in the UK will handle this particular conflict between its established position and that predominant within the EU is interesting and important. One prediction is that it will maintain its current policy of encouraging the employee involvement concept as opposed to the EU employee participation concept, and will perceive any concession to the latter as a 'concession' to the labour movement, only to be made for strategic reasons when under considerable industrial and/or political pressure. Since some of the employee participation approaches in other EU countries are neither out of sympathy with current British Labour Party (and Liberal Democrat) policy, nor apparently in conflict with the perspective of the leaders of some large trade unions in the UK, then a welcome for any such Conservative 'concessions' to employee participation could be expected from influential sections of the leadership of the labour movement.

However, a case can be argued that any such developments could turn out to be disastrous for the trade union rank and file, with the emergence of employee participation – sanctioned by influential leaders of the labour movement – as subversive of trade union independence. Such developments could very well open up even more opportunities for UK employers to introduce just-in-time, greater flexibility of labour, total quality initiatives, teamworking, and perhaps even more single union deals. Despite trends in recent years in many EU states, not least the UK, of increasingly decentralised industrial relations and an increasingly fragmented labour movement, in the event of economic upswing the 'concession' of employee participation might be made to the labour movement in the UK, and the emergence of a new 'European corporatism' should not be entirely ruled out in an attempt to stifle trade union ability to use industrial action in its battles against multinational company power in Europe.

Japanese business interests and EU economic integration

Comment was made previously about the determination of Japanese big business not to be shut out of Fortress Europe and the significance of Japanese investment in the UK (chapter one). The indications are that Japanese big business will widen its campaign over the next decade to increase its market share in Western Europe, particularly (but not only) in motor vehicles and consumer electronics – and the chances of it having success in this respect seem high. Increasing economic integration of the EU is greatly intensifying competition in most product markets. The impact of serious Japanese economic intervention will further intensify competition, which in turn is likely to force firms under threat to reassess their methods of operation. The extent to which the winning companies in the race for market share have made use of such new management initiatives as just-in-

Prospects for Japanese investment in the UK

In the financial year ending March 1989 direct investment by Japanese companies in the UK was £2.3 billion. Nomura Research Institute Europe estimated (August 1989) that annual foreign direct investment in Britain by Japanese companies could reach £6.5 billion by the end of the 1990s.[8]

time, greater flexibility of labour, employee involvement, total quality management and teamworking, will influence the speed and extent to which their competitors follow suit and also develop such new management methods. Japanese companies in motor vehicles and consumer electronics, of course, embrace these methods.

The Japanese car plants in the UK are the Nissan, Toyota and Honda sites, at Sunderland, Burnaston near Derby and Swindon respectively. Nissan has plans for expansion of its existing production, though with some caution in light of recession, whilst Toyota and Honda also have their production facilities in operation. Toyota has an engine plant operating in Clwyd, North Wales. Honda began production at an engine plant at Swindon in 1989. The latter has been involved in joint operations at Rover's Longbridge site, Birmingham, since 1979 as a result of a licensing agreement with Rover. There was a 20 per cent equity swap between Honda and Rover in April 1990. However, in 1994 Rover was sold to BMW, and whilst the 20% equity swap will be dismantled, licensing arrangements for design, development etc will remain. Less attention has been drawn to the former Bedford van plant at Luton, now known as IBC Vehicles. Ownership of IBC is in the joint hands of General Motors (60 per cent) and the Japanese firm Isuzu (40 per cent).[9] Japanese motor vehicle companies are attempting to develop investment elsewhere in the EU – Suzuki in Spain (with Santana), Mitsubishi in the Netherlands (with Volvo), Mazda with Ford, and Daihatsu, Nissan and Toyota in several minor light commercial vehicle projects – but none of these initiatives represent anything like the concentration of investment by Japanese motor vehicle companies in the UK. A discouraging UK domestic market for cars in recent years has left the Japanese investors undeterred, since their intention was never to target the UK market in particular, but markets across the EU.

The European Commission has been forced to address two fundamental questions on this issue: the threat to EU companies from cars manufactured at Japanese-owned sites within the EU and the threat to EU companies from Japanese imports. In July 1991, the EU drew up an agreement with

Japan, which placed certain limits on the extent of its operations in the EU until the end of 1999. Under this agreement Japanese companies are restricted to a maximum market share of 16 per cent. Direct import of cars from Japan is restricted to the 1991 figure of 1.2 million. Cars imported from Japan will continue to be subject to quotas in the UK, Spain, France, Italy and Portugal. Manufacture of Japanese models in Europe is subject to an informal understanding that this too will not exceed 1.2 million cars per year.[10]

Since combined productive capacity for the mid-1990s of the three greenfield Nissan, Toyota and Honda sites in the UK is around 500,000 vehicles, and Japanese investment in the EU is concentrated in the UK, these limits seem to give the Japanese car companies considerable further scope even in the short term, and plenty of scope after 1999. If such Japanese investment continues to be concentrated in the UK, then these EU limits are not likely to slow down Japanese economic intervention here.

Recent trends in car sales in Western Europe

In addition to the effects on most sections of industry of greater economic integration within the EU, the car industry in the Union faces a number of other current problems. Sales figures for recent years for Western Europe have put car manufacturers into two distinct divisions, with Volkswagen, Fiat, General Motors, Ford, Peugeot and Renault all clearly in the first division, and with Mercedes-Benz, Nissan, BMW, Toyota, Rover, Mazda, Volvo, Mitsubishi and Honda clearly in the second division.[12] In most West European countries car sales demonstrated a serious decline in the early 1990s, but there were also some uneven developments in the markets. The German market experienced considerable growth temporarily as a result of reunification, and Volkswagen, General Motors and Ford gained as a result. The UK and Spanish markets demonstrated a marked decline in the same period. Ford experienced heavy financial losses; the UK is Ford's biggest market in Europe and it had its worst result here in 1990 for 20 years. Fiat faces difficulty because of excessive concentration on its own Italian market, with its profits halved in 1992 for the motor vehicle side of its business.[13] By 1993 the UK economy appeared to be taking its first faltering steps out of recession, with its car industry leading the way. Unfortunately, this coincided with key EU economies facing still growing problems of recession, and therefore placing major obstacles in the way of UK car exports to important EU markets.[11]

The prospect of a dramatic rationalisation of the car industry in Europe

A dramatic rationalisation of the car industry in Western Europe in the 1990s, encouraged by increasing economic integration of the EU, is a serious and not particularly surprising possibility. Since the car and consumer electronics industries are the flagship for the new management techniques, what would be the implications if this did occur? Car companies will not be able to stand still either in terms of cost-cutting methods or more effective means of meeting customer satisfaction. Further exploitation of just-in-time and wider application of *kaizen* principles could be expected. The latter may prove to be more important than the former, since it is a *learning philosophy* and could ultimately bring about yet further dramatic changes in management methods beyond just-in-time. The current battle between Nissan and Toyota for Japan's domestic market may indicate the future direction of management methods in the car industry. One of several possibilities is the combination of just-in-time with a much greater level of investment in new technology than seen to date.

The recession

The economic recession in the UK which commenced in late 1990 or early 1991 has been more serious than the early 1980s recession.

Statistics which demonstrate the emergence of the recession also demonstrate both the international character of the recession and that the consequences for the UK economy were much worse in the early 1990s than for most industrial countries.[14] The uncontentious explanation for this latter point is that it is because of the particular characteristics of the UK economy; the Labour Party's and Liberal Democrats' argument is that it is also because of Conservative government policy.

The plight of investment in manufacturing in the UK is obviously a very important part of the problem. In a critical period of recession between 1990 and 1992, manufacturing investment fell by a third, with output down by 10 per cent and employment reduced by 600,000.[15] Such a collapse of manufacturing is not simply an indicator of the extent of recession, it is also a potentially serious obstacle to effective economy recovery. In the event of an upturn in the economy, UK manufacturing may be unable to meet demand, resulting in increased imports of manufactured goods and a further deterioration in the balance of trade.[16] There is good reason to see this as a serious problem for the economy, though it is possible that it may be offset to a degree by the productive capacity of Japanese manufacturers based in the UK, particularly the car industry. Such car manufacturers may be well poised to benefit from any economic upswing in other EU economies, to expand exports from the UK and therefore to assist UK balance of trade figures.[17] Conversely, time may prove that delayed, prolonged recession in other key European economies is critical in discouraging economic recovery in the UK.

Persistently high unemployment in spite of economic recovery is likely to be another problem. Even in the event of an impressive economic recovery in the 1990s, a major impact on unemployment (eg, reducing the figures to one million) seems unlikely. Following the early 1980s recession, whilst official unemployment figures dropped considerably, they never returned to anything like the late 1970s levels. In any case, the figures in the 1980s were also affected by numerous changes to the way in which the figures were calculated, almost all of which produced a more favourable result for the Conservative government. The growth of the *new* management initiatives by employers is likely to be an important factor in discouraging any economic recovery from creating a major reduction in unemployment levels. The growth of numerical, functional and temporal labour flexibility has an important part to play here. With increased functional flexibility established through radical changes to working practices and the breakdown of demarcation between jobs (in both manufacturing and private and public service sectors), fewer workers are required and productivity is increased. As recession bites, an employer can implement redundancies, and exploit the climate of fear to impose radical changes in working practices on the remaining workforce. This in turn may provide the employer with the necessary productive capacity to respond to the economic upturn and increased demand when it comes. The employer *may* take on *some* new labour when the recovery comes, but if so it certainly will not amount to a return to pre-recession levels, and then will only occur when the employer is quite confident that the recovery is established. There can also be considerable advantages to employers of a combined strategy of functional, numerical and temporal flexibility of labour in these circumstances. The use of a pool of part-time and/or temporary labour and more flexible working hours arrangements, in conjunction with radical changes to working practices, can not only provide many employers with the ability to respond to an economic upturn and increased demand without any significant increase in labour, but can also protect them against a 'false start' to recovery or short-lived future economic growth.

Another factor which may discourage a fall in unemployment in spite of economic recovery is that where manufacturing is managing to survive and develop in the UK, it may well be increasingly capital intensive rather than labour intensive. All this, of course, is quite apart from the possible opportunities provided to employers by the recession to impose total quality systems, and thus to achieve cost reductions and productivity improvements.[18] These initiatives may make their mark too in discouraging an increased demand for labour in spite of an increased demand for goods and services in the event of economic recovery. The exploitation of the recession by employers to impose such *new* management initiatives, and the prospect of little reduction in unemployment levels in spite of economic recovery, certainly poses disturbing challenges to the trade union movement in the UK in the 1990s.

A prolonged crisis in public spending in the 1990s also seems likely not least because of the prospect of persistently high levels of unemployment. In fact, an upturn in the economy could be paralleled by increasing unemployment. This could occur because of continuing radical advances in labour flexibility by employers, the expansion of capital intensive as opposed to labour intensive industries and a time lag in any response of labour demand to economic recovery.

This is the context, of further severe rounds of public spending cuts, in which the public sector initiatives of increased privatisation, implementation of the Citizen's Charter, total quality initiatives, the development of human resource management techniques, the increasing application of performance indicators, the growth of labour flexibility and growing confrontation with public sector trade unions need to be seen. To attempt to analyse new management initiatives in the public sector in isolation from such factors is likely to produce misleading conclusions.

The challenge to union bargaining power posed by recession and high unemployment is likely to be a more significant factor than anti-union legislation in bringing about the growth of new management initiatives in the UK. The 1990s recession and its associated increase in unemployment means a surplus of labour in many sections of the economy, which undermines trade union bargaining power. And union bargaining power is likely to be further undermined in these circumstances because many of those in work are affected by the fear of losing their jobs, and are less likely to take the risks of confrontation with management. Indeed the latter may be more significant than the former. A prolonged recession or faltering recovery will probably provide employers with a number of important opportunities for the extension of new management initiatives in the UK.

Employers' attempts to increase further the flexibility of labour seem likely. In the early 1980s recession, there was a trend – particularly in the chemicals industry – towards 'blockbuster' deals on labour flexibility, particularly in the form of radical changes to working practices. Throughout manufacturing generally, however, there are some doubts about quite how much employers actually achieved in real terms in respect of such change in working practices. By late 1990, the onset of the recession in the UK, quite a number of employers had won wide-ranging enabling agreements which included trade union acceptance of the principle of extensive functional flexibility of labour, but there is good reason for scepticism about the extent to which these had been implemented. However, a prolonged period of recession and economic insecurity could change all that. It may mean that such agreements will be implemented with a vengeance, and that more employers will go for new 'blockbuster' deals incorporating widespread labour flexibility. Such new deals may not only include extensive functional flexibility, but also temporal and numerical flexibility.

However, it is important to see the impact on employers of a deep and prolonged recession in a broader context. A prolonged period of economic uncertainty will place severe financial pressures on both private and public sector employers, which will force them to carry out a relentless search to reduce costs. Wage costs are an obvious target, and greater labour flexibility is one way to achieve this. (Others are through lower wage settlements and through more job losses.) Just-in-time methods of production and associated teamworking and total quality management systems can also provide ample opportunities for employers to reduce costs, and serious recession in the UK might be expected to increase the adoption of such methods by employers. Employers in manufacturing who have not previously taken just-in-time methods seriously may come under particular pressure. And the next new management initiative which unions in the public service sector may witness – on top of increased labour flexibility, total quality and Citizen's Charter initiatives, and employee involvement and human resource management techniques – may be the application of the just-in-time philosophy to their non-manufacturing areas of work, particularly to administration.

There is a strong argument to suggest that just-in-time will become a much more prominent issue for industrial relations generally in the 1990s. If this is so, it raises the important question of how UK management will attempt to solve the problem of just-in-time's vulnerability to strike action. In the 1980s UK employers who were at the forefront in introducing just-in-time, did so in conjunction with extensive employee involvement programmes, aimed to change the culture of the workplace from an emphasis on conflict between workforce and management to an emphasis on worker-management co-operation and apparent common interests. Whilst it is questionable how effective employee involvement programmes have been, it is clear that their intention when introduced in conjunction with just-in-time has been to reduce the latter's vulnerability to strike action. However, high unemployment in the 1980s, and fear of redundancy, and to a lesser extent anti-union legislation, have been important in reducing union bargaining power and union ability and/or willingness to organise effective industrial action. As a result, employers keen to introduce just-in-time in the 1980s have been less anxious than they might have been about the vulnerability of just-in-time to strike action. The important point which arises from this is that, whilst employers may be able to get away with a much more widespread introduction of just-in-time in the course of the 1990s recession, they will still be forced to seek a more stable and permanent solution in the UK to the problem of just-in-time's intrinsic vulnerability to industrial action. Therefore, employers might be expected to attempt to establish much more extensive and effective employee involvement programmes during the recession in readiness to help protect just-in-time in the future from the vulnerability of strike action, but it is questionable whether this in itself will be sufficient.

Future direction of Conservative government policy

Any continuation of Conservative government in the UK in the 1990s is likely to contribute to the further development of new management initiatives in various ways.

The extension of privatisation is a publicly stated objective of Conservative policy. We can expect to see further attempts at the privatisation of large scale nationalised industries and at partial privatisation of the kind associated with the NHS and education. The development of compulsory competitive tendering and market testing may be more inhibited because of potential legal hurdles for the government. (See chapter one for a detailed account of these issues.) The future trajectory of privatisation and the further development of business philosophy and methods within the remaining public sector, however, cannot be separated from public spending cuts and the predicted size of the Public Sector Borrowing Requirement for the remainder of the decade. Privatisation and cuts, on the basis of Conservative policy, will continue to be important in the promotion of new management initiatives because they encourage increased flexibility of labour, the implementation of total quality programmes, performance indicators, employee appraisal and performance related pay, increased productivity and more effective competition. The implementation of plans to dismantle the little which still remains of a unified public sector would pose greater challenges to union organisation as the decade unfolds.

Just as Conservative policy is committed to the extension of privatisation, so too is it committed to a continuing programme of anti-union legislation for the foreseeable future. There may be dangers, however, in overestimating the extent to which unions' determination to organise industrial action continues to be affected by this kind of legislation. Whilst the prospect of direct confrontation by unions with the law on a national scale subsided in the mid-1980s, many trade unionists seem to have developed ever more imaginative ways of organising effective industrial action when real support from the union membership for such action has been there, in spite of anti-union legislation.

In their 1992 General Election manifesto the Conservatives emphasised that the number of days lost each year from strikes had fallen from an average 12.9 million in the 1970s to less than a million in 1991 – the lowest figure since records began a century earlier.[19] Whilst this statement is correct, too many assumptions should not be made about the importance of anti-union legislation in bringing this about. It is important to note, for example, that strike activity in the three other largest European Union states (France, Germany and Italy) has also declined quite dramatically since 1979, yet these countries have substantially wider rights for unions to organise and take strike action than in the UK.[20] Care should therefore be taken not to over-emphasise new anti-union legislation as a factor in encouraging the further development of new management initiatives in the 1990s.

The alternative? – Labour Party and Liberal Democrat policy

Not only is the political challenge to the Labour Party in the 1990s very considerable, so too is the economic challenge to Labour in government. Failure to return the economy to full employment or to radically reduce

> **The 1992 Conservative Party manifesto's proposals for anti-union legislation: implemented by the 1993 Trade Union Reform and Employment Rights Act**
>
> - We will make automatic deduction of union membership dues without written authorisation unlawful.
> - We will take measures to give individuals greater freedom in choosing a union.
> - We will legislate to require that all pre-strike ballots are postal and subject to independent scrutiny, and that at least seven days' notice of a strike is given after a ballot.
> - People who use public services will have the right to restrain the disruption of those services by unlawful industrial action.[21]

unemployment levels (likely given current political trends) will act as a restraint on union bargaining power, and significant public spending cuts or restraints are likely to remain on the agenda. The continuation of high unemployment levels and on-going public spending cuts/restraints allow and encourage both private and public sector employers to develop the new management initiatives.

The desire to win business confidence, and the promotion of the concept of industrial partnership, have been a central feature of Labour's policy towards industry in recent years. Implicit in this approach is a determination to emphasise co-operation and common ground between trade unions and employers – effectively, 'if there is a failure to achieve business growth and a better ability to compete, then we all lose'. This approach to industrial policy has important implications for the development of new management initiatives.

Unlike the Conservatives, Labour believes that business cannot achieve its goals without some kind of support and encouragement from the state. This approach will also have a number of important implications for employers keen to develop new management initiatives.

Labour policy implications for just-in-time and teamworking

Labour Party policy implies an essentially non-interventionist approach towards just-in-time and teamworking management initiatives, and is supportive of management freedom to take such initiatives if they are important in improving the competitiveness of their company or organisation. Central to Labour policy is a determination to win business

161

confidence, particularly by means of its policies on investment, interest rates, inflation, training, new technology, the EU, employment legislation and its concept of a partnership between government and industry. For a Labour government to intervene in industry in any way to encourage trade unions to oppose just-in-time or teamworking initiatives, or to encourage unions to exact too high a price for their introduction, would be seen by many companies as an obstacle to employers' attempts to improve their competitiveness and would contribute to undermining business confidence in that Labour government. A Labour government could be reasonably expected to view just-in-time and teamworking as in the realm of those matters which can best be dealt with by those parties with the expertise in industrial relations at the workplace, and in their own way.

In the case of teamworking in particular, it is worth examining the significance of Labour's concept of partnership in industry. Teamworking is a very important vehicle for the introduction of several of the new management methods. It can be used to establish a just-in-time system, with its associated total quality management, and in conjunction with extensive functional flexibility of labour and employee involvement methods and philosophy. The concept of the team is one which employee involvement advocates aim to promote at various levels within a company. Labour policy tends to favour a European-style employee participation philosophy, rather than the management-dominated UK employee involvement concept. Nevertheless, such promotion of employee participation, in conjunction with Labour's concept of partnership in industry, is likely to encourage a political climate favourable to the introduction of teamworking.

Labour Party policy and single union deals

It remains to be seen whether 'single union no strike agreements, which caused so much discord within the trade union movement in the 1980s, will increase or decrease in significance as an issue in UK industrial relations as we approach the year 2000. Whether in government or in opposition, however, the experience of the 1980s suggests that the Labour Party will make no intervention, verbally or otherwise, in the event of future trade union disputes about the signing of single union no-strike deals. It perceives this as the prerogative of the trade union movement. At the same time, any statement by the Labour Party leadership which favoured single union no-strike deals would be surprising, since this might provoke serious public criticism from the leadership of several large unions with which it enjoys a relatively loyal relationship.

Labour Party policy and labour flexibility in the workplace

Three aspects of Labour Party policy which are relevant to numerical, functional and temporal labour flexibility initiatives are training, legal rights in the workplace and compulsory competitive tendering in public services.

Increased government support for training for school-leavers, unemployed and employed people has been an often emphasised aspect of the Labour Party's programme. Workplace training, of course, has a key role to play in relation to increased functional flexibility of labour. In the present economic climate it is certainly difficult for trade unions to persuade their employers to retrain workers rather than make them redundant when company reorganisation or 'rationalisation' takes place. In a redundancy situation, the company's plan will often be to establish a much wider flexibility of working practices amongst the remaining workforce. For this to be done *effectively*, expenditure on training of one form or another will be necessary. Also it is common for management to attempt to develop their programme of increased functional flexibility of labour over a period of time by stealth, or as part of a series of package deals which link changes in working practices to pay deals; this is then often followed by redundancies. Again, for this strategy to work in management terms, carefully planned expenditure on training could be expected to be a significant issue. However, it may be that many employers are implementing such increased flexibility initiatives without increased per capita training costs, because of short term planning processes and 'fire-fighting' management – management may take further major initiatives within the workplace, for different and changing purposes, before the ill-effects of inadequate retraining have a chance to become too conspicuous.

Whatever the reality under Conservative governments of the 1980s and 1990s in respect of the significance of training in relation to increased functional flexibility, there are grounds to argue that Labour's ideas on workplace training will at least assist companies in the introduction of increased functional flexibility of labour.

Conversely, Labour's policy regarding employment protection legislation and compulsory competitive tendering is generally discouraging of the growth of numerical flexibility of labour .[22] Labour have stated that,

Our Charter for Employees will cover equal status in law for all employees, including part-time, temporary, casual and homeworkers, a minimum hourly wage... full protection against unfair dismissal and provide rights to both men and women so as to reconcile their work and family responsibilities.[23]

The implementation of this policy faces employers with certain legal obstacles to the operation of a numerically flexible labour force. Placing restrictions on the extent of numerical flexibility of labour may seem at variance with the implications of Labour Party policy for most of the new management initiatives. It does relate logically, however, to a particular underlying principle of Labour Party economic and industrial policy, in addition to the workers' rights question. Numerical flexibility is linked all too often to short-term business strategies, whilst an underlying principle of Labour policy has been to take initiatives to encourage long-term business planning.

Labour has also declared plans to abolish compulsory competitive tendering in both the National Health Service and local government.[24] Cleaning the interior of NHS and local government buildings has been an especially lucrative target for private contractors under the compulsory competitive tendering regime. It has been overwhelmingly women workers, already employed on poor pay and conditions prior to tendering, who have suffered particularly from the use of numerical flexibility of labour by private cleaning contractors. In the event of abolition of compulsory competitive tendering, the growth of numerical flexibility of labour in local government and the NHS would be significantly discouraged. However, both the NHS and local government are likely to remain under considerable pressure to minimise costs in light of on-going restraints on public expenditure as a whole. Such cost restraints may have the effect of partially offsetting the discouragement of numerical flexibility of labour in NHS and local government services as a result of the abolition of compulsory competitive tendering.

Labour Party policy and employee involvement and participation

The Labour Party has made clear its commitment to encourage employee participation in a form more akin to European Union models rather than the British Conservative concept of employee involvement.[25] Employee involvement is more about management initiatives which inform and consult the workforce but which avoid any kind of participation in management decision-making, and is based on a voluntary approach

The Labour Party on Employee Participation

Giving individuals more say in decisions at work can make a major contribution to economic efficiency as well as to individuals' quality of life – as experienced in Germany, Sweden and other successful countries successfully demonstrates. Over time this participation will increase the influence of employees within a company. It will also increase their sense of responsibility and commitment to the company.[26]

rather than on imposition by government. The Labour Party's approach, however, might well be seen as providing a toe-hold in management decision-making – although Labour would probably argue that it is an approach which will allow for more effective use of workforce expertise to make better management decisions from which both employer and employees gain.[27] A criticism from the left of the labour movement is that this approach has no real potential as a serious challenge to managerial authority, whilst at the same time it lends credibility to management decisions which may very well be contrary to the interests and influence of organised labour. In other words, whilst participation may provide some gain for unions – in terms of information, for example – the price which employers could exact for this in respect of loss of trade union independence could be even greater than in the case of current British-style employee involvement.

The Labour Party has related the concept of employee participation to a wide range of important issues, including health and safety, training, the working environment, pension schemes, flexible hours packages, child care arrangements, plant closures, large-scale redundancies, guidelines on new technology, major training initiatives, and take-overs and mergers.[28] It is, however, unclear whether Labour Party policy intends to promote employee participation based on trade union representatives or *employee* representatives.[29] The concept of employee representation cuts across traditional trade union recognition and negotiating practice in the UK, which accepts the right of the recognised union to select its representatives in the way it thinks fit, and for management to deal only with the recognised union. Employee representation is incorporated in the Nissan-style agreements in the UK and in several EU countries' employee participation schemes.

The distinction between trade union and employee representation apart, the logic of Labour's support for the concept of employee participation can

165

be related to the concessions it has made since 1979 to individualist ideology. One view of the post-1979 era is as a battle between individualist and collectivist ideologies, with serious defeats inflicted on the latter. Thatcherism is said to have championed the rights of small businesspeople, homeowners, the 'moderate' trade unionists who made up the 'silent majority', in opposition to the faceless bureaucracies of the nationalised industries and public services, and the 'undemocratic, militant' trade unions. Particularly in the area of employment legislation, Labour has made certain significant concessions to the Conservative view. Whilst the Labour Party has declared its opposition to Conservative legislation on secondary (sympathy) industrial action and other areas where the collective rights of trade unions have been withdrawn by Conservative governments, Labour policy has emphasised individual legal rights of employees. This is demonstrated not only by Labour's policy of improving employment protection rights, but also by Labour's policy of retaining the trade union balloting principles first introduced by the Conservatives' 1984 Trade Union Act.

The Citizen's Charter is another example of Conservative individualist ideology, heralded as championing the patients', parents' and other public service users' rights. The Labour Party policy response has been the production of its own version of a citizen's charter and, like the Conservatives, it has apparently become an advocate of total quality systems within the public services. Whilst trade unions are built on the concept of collectivism, Labour Party policy has increasingly made concessions to individualist ideology at the expense of collectivism. The Labour Party's espousal of employee participation can usefully be seen in the context of its increased sympathy with individualist ideology.

The Labour Party and total quality initiatives

If Labour Party policy is conducive to the introduction of just-in-time and teamworking in industry, by implication it will encourage total quality initiatives of one form or another (plus continuous improvement philosophy) because these are an integral part of just-in-time.

Total quality initiatives are also likely to be encouraged by Labour Party policy in respect of the public service sector for other reasons. Serious recession in the UK economy has brought with it substantial increases in unemployment, which can be expected to extend beyond an upturn in the economy. Such unemployment means both reduced revenue and increased expenditure for government at the same time. It seems likely that a public spending crisis of considerably greater proportions than that experienced in the 1980s will dominate the 1990s decade in the UK. In such circumstances , the Labour Party in government faces a very serious problem regarding the management of public services. How can it spend less (or at best restrain public expenditure) whilst at the same time improving the quality of service to the public? This is precisely the question which total quality initiatives in the public service sector address.

The Labour Party has done little to provoke public debate about quality. It has not demonstrated a recognition of different concepts of quality,[30] nor has it challenged the underlying assumptions of the Conservatives' concept of quality in the public service sector. It has failed to put forward a clear alternative concept of quality which builds and unites both the demands of the community and of public service workers, rather than the approach promoted by the Conservatives which potentially stimulates the demands of the community at the expense of the working conditions of public service employees. Whether it be total quality management, BS 5750, the 'Investors in People' quality standards approach, or variations or developments of these, Labour Party policy does not imply any radical departure from these types of initiatives in the public services, which have already been promoted under Conservative governments.

Liberal Democrat policy

Implicit in Liberal Democrat policy is recognition of the need of employers to apply increasingly such new management methods as just-in-time production, teamworking and functional and temporal flexibility of labour.[31] Like the Labour Party, the Liberal Democrats are critical of numerical flexibility of labour. They were in favour of the Social Chapter and, for example, support the application of full-time workers' employment protection rights to part-timers and homeworkers on a pro-rata basis.[32] Also like the Labour Party, they advocate an emphasis on training for employees and are critical of 'short-termism' in the workplace.

However, Liberal Democrat policy in respect of new management initiatives places especial emphasis on employee participation, as opposed to employee involvement. The Liberal Democrats' concept also includes legal rights for employees to participate in profit sharing and share ownership schemes. The Liberal Democrat approach to employee participation is part of a fairly comprehensive policy which places human resource management at the centre of new management initiatives. This is consistent with the individualist ideological traditions of the Liberal Party, and its commitment to the promotion of co-operation between employees and management at work.

There are aspects of Liberal Democrat policy which pose a serious challenge to trade union interests. In respect of employee participation it advocates the idea of *employee*, as opposed to trade union, representatives, to be elected to the 'employee committees' which are an important part of its participation concept. This could compete with and challenge established trade union negotiating structures, and effectively erects a parallel structure to the latter. The Liberal Democrats defend their policy by arguing that if a union is performing a useful function for the workforce, it is likely that many of the employee representatives will also be prominent figures in their union.[33]

On the question of single union agreements, Liberal Democrat policy is to encourage such deals, and also to favour such techniques as pendulum arbitration. At the same time the right to strike is not ruled out altogether. 'The right to withdrawal of labour in pursuit of a justified dispute is as fundamental a right as any other; in the last resort, unions and individuals must possess the right to organise and take strike action.'[34] In addition, 'It should be stressed that we are not in general proposing to repeal the union legislation passed by the Conservative Governments of the last eleven (*sic*) years.'[35]

Some conclusions

There is a significant area of common ground between the policy of the main political parties in relation to the development of new management initiatives in 1990s. There is full agreement in principle that government needs to do what it can to encourage UK employers to adopt and develop the new management techniques and philosophies in order to compete more effectively, particularly internationally. The areas of difference between the main political parties concern the detail of how this might be done and the view each takes of *particular* new management initiatives.

Unlike the Conservatives, the Labour and Liberal Democrat Parties are critical of numerical flexibility of labour. The Labour Party and the Liberal Democrats also believe that employers must place much more emphasis on training than they have done under Conservative governments, which in turn may have implications for more effective functional flexibility of labour. The Labour Party and Liberal Democrats' approach to employee involvement and participation also differs from the Conservatives in that the former favour employee *participation* as opposed to the employee involvement concept which emphasises information and consultation alone, provided by employers on a voluntary basis. The Liberal Democrats also emphasise the role of employees as individuals and advocate employee 'financial participation' in the workplace. Like the Conservatives, the Liberal Democrats believe in encouragement for single union deals.

There is strong evidence to suggest that emergence from recession in the UK will not bring with it a *radical* reduction in unemployment. Increased flexibility of labour may play an important part in creating this situation. If this is the case, then on-going high unemployment may continue to restrict the bargaining power of trade unions. Therefore emergence from the UK recession may not make it any easier for trade unions to resist new management initiatives, even if they choose to do so. The role of public expenditure crises in promoting the development of new management initiatives in the public sector is unlikely to disappear in the near future. Central to this is the search by the main political parties for solutions to the problem of how the costs of public services can be cut whilst at the same time the public can be satisfied that the quality of services provided are being improved.

European restructuring of industrial, service and commercial sectors, extensive European mergers and take-overs, and growing Japanese investment in cars and consumer electronics concentrated in the UK, all associated with the development of the EU, are part of a considerable intensification of international competition. The immense, complex obstacles to extensive exploitation of markets in Eastern Europe and the former Soviet states, combined with the implications of a disjointed pattern of recession in Europe, may further emphasise the battle for market share and intensification of competition. This range of factors may force employers to apply and develop new management techniques more extensively and in an increasingly aggressive manner, as part of an increasingly fierce battle to survive.

Notes

1 Paulo Cecchini *et al, The European Challenge – 1992 – the benefits of a single market,* European Commission, 1986, English edition, Gower, 1988.
2 'Capitalism cannot unite Europe', Pat Craven, *Militant,* 9.12.88, p8.
3 John Carvel, 'EC plans "minimal" rule changes on jobs', *The Guardian,* 21.7.93, p6.
4 Paulo Cecchini, *op cit*
5 As referred to in Pat Craven, *op cit*

6 Greg Coyne and Mike O'Neill, *1992, The Single European Market – Information and Analysis for Trade Unionists*, Merseyside Trade Union, Community and Unemployed Resource Centre.

7 For more detail see, for example, IDS European Report No. 358, October 1991, pp9-12, and Sylvia Schloss, 'Carrot or Club', *Industrial Society Magazine*, September 1990, pp9-13.

8 Christopher McCooey and Tim Hindle, 'Japanese Investment – A Mixed Blessing for the UK?', *Eurobusiness*, January 1990, p34.

9 Kevin Done, 'Crash Course', *International Management*, September 1991, p72.

10 *Ibid*, p73. Japanese car companies' market share in the EU in 1992 was 11.3 per cent, Simon Beavis, 'Europe's car firms seek freeze at 11.3% on Japanese imports', *The Guardian*, 13.7.93.

11 *Ibid*, pp70-72.

12 For example, sales figures for 1991 for Western Europe were as follows: Volkswagen, Fiat, General Motors, Ford, Peugeot and Renault each sold between approximately 700,000 and 1.2 million cars; Mercedes-Benz, Nissan, BMW, Toyota, Rover, Mazda, Volvo, Mitsubishi and Honda each sold between approximately 70,000 and 240,000 cars. Source: Beavis, *op cit.*

13 Tony Bosworth, 'The Motor Industry – Potholes Down Recovery Road', *Investors Chronicle*, 16.7.93, p65.

14 See, for example, Michael Roberts, 'The end of the upswing', *Militant International Review*, Issue 45, New Year 1991, pp32-3.

15 Peter Taaffe, 'Prospects for Britain under Major', *Militant International Review*, Issue 48, Summer 1992, p5.

16 *Ibid.*

17 See, for example, John Campbell, 'Britain's Renascent Car Industry', *Investors' Chronicle*, 20.4.90, pp16-17.

18 It should be pointed out, however, that increased introduction of total quality systems by employers will not necessarily result from the recession, and the converse is possible.

19 The Conservative Party, *The Best Future for Britain – The Conservative Manifesto 1992*, p20.

20 *Labour Research*, 'Twisting the Knife', August 1991, pp5-8, and the Department of Employment *Gazette*, December 1990.

21 The Conservative Party Manifesto, *op cit*, p20.

22 This is also consistent with Labour's support for the Social Chapter.

23 The Labour Party, 'Opportunity Britain', *Labour Party News*, No25, July-August 1991, p26.

24 The Labour Party has suggested only one minor exception to its plans to abolish compulsory competitive tendering. Only where local government services have consistently failed to meet a proper standard will local authorities have to put the work up for tender, and even then various restrictions will apply including contract compliance. Source: 'Opportunity Britain', see previous note.

25 For example, see the Labour Party, 'Meet the Challenge, Make the Change – Final Report of Labour's Policy Review for the 1990s', 1989, p25.

26 Labour's concept of employee participation is similar to that of Bryan Stevens, director of the Involvement and Participation Association. See chapter 3 for more information on Bryan Stevens' view of employee participation and involvement.

27 The Labour Party, 'Meet the Challenge…', *op cit.*

28 *Ibid.*

29 In the case of occupational pensions, for example, it does state that workers will have a real say in the management of their pensions funds through the election of *trade union representatives*. However, in other areas of industrial relations a Labour government might

encourage *employee* representation.

30 See, for example, the explanations and arguments about different concepts of quality in Naomi Pfeffer and Anna Coote, *Is Quality Good for You? – A critical review of quality assurance in welfare services*, Social Policy Paper No5, Institute for Public Policy Research, 1991.

31 Liberal Democrats, *Citizens at Work – Federal Green Paper No16*, 1990.

32 *Ibid*, p26.

33 *Ibid*, p22.

34 *Ibid*, p24.

35 *Ibid*, p22.

Chapter 7

Problems and opportunities for management and unions

Much of this book has been devoted to an explanation of the main new management initiatives and techniques in the UK, and how they operate in practice. An effort has been made to clarify the relationship between each of the new management initiatives and techniques, and to explain the dependency of certain initiatives on others. Attention has been drawn to the significance of a range of national and international factors, currently and historically, which act as the driving force behind the diffusion and implementation of these new management initiatives.

The debate about whether such developments can be characterised as post-Fordist has been deliberately avoided in the preceding pages, and is outside the scope of this book. For the record, the underlying assumption has been that there is insufficient evidence to conclude that a fundamentally different form of organisation of work is emerging (ie, post-Fordism), which is essentially distinct from Fordist mass production-orientated organisation of work, characteristic of the 1950s and 1960s. The stark polarisation between Fordism and post-Fordism is seen as too simplistic, and the concept of post-Fordism is not considered a useful one in terms of its ability to explain the processes taking place.[1] This is not to suggest that the new management initiatives considered are perceived as being little more than some passing management fad. They are perceived as being part of significant international developments in management thinking and ideas, spreading well beyond the car and consumer electronics industries in which many of them were initially developed. In fact, they are seen to present a challenge of major proportions to the traditional outlook and practice of both management and trade unions in the UK.

In conclusion, two broad questions seem particularly important. First, does management in the UK have the ability to implement widely and effectively a programme of new management initiatives and techniques in industrial and service sectors beyond the cars and consumer electronics industries? Second, are these new management initiatives and techniques a *major* problem for the trade unions, and in any event how will the unions respond?

Management weaknesses

In respect of management's ability to implement a programme of new management initiatives there are several areas of doubt. Certainly in the car, consumer electronics and associated supplier industries, in spite of key problems still to be resolved, programmes of new management initiatives are relatively well advanced by UK standards. It is in other areas of manufacturing, and the private and public service sectors, not least the latter, where the more serious problems for management lie. Five common weaknesses of management are apparent.

i. *The piecemeal or 'add-on' approach to new management initiatives* still seems popular amongst many sections of management in the UK. In the early 1980s there was a lot of management interest in quality circles. These were seen essentially as the key to the success of Japanese industry, and were commonly implemented by management in the UK in isolation of other initiatives. Most of them failed as a result. In spite of this, the 'add-on' approach still seems to be practiced by many sections of management, rather than the adoption of an integrated strategy. This appears to indicate a failure on the part of management to understand the interrelationship of the various new management initiatives and techniques. It is also related to other management weaknesses.

ii. *Is management prepared to change sufficiently itself* to enable the success of new management initiative programmes? Employee involvement and teamworking, for example, can entail fundamental changes to management structures and patterns of authority. Managers may lose the control they have exercised over particular groups of employees, and a major element of uncertainty is injected into the situation. It may mean that some employees who have criticised particular managers for years finally get their way. In short, key elements of new management initiative programmes can threaten traditional management interests at all levels, and may place the jobs of some managers on the line. There has to be doubt about the extent to which current UK management in many sectors are prepared to accept this. There is therefore a degree of management vested interest in the 'add-on' approach to the implementation of new management initiatives and techniques, and particularly when it is coupled to short-term strategies.

iii. Criticism of *the 'short-termism' of British industry* raises important questions. Short-term approaches of one kind or another are evident in the investment policies of British industry, in the strategic planning of many companies, in the implementation of new management initiatives programmes themselves, and in the personal career strategies of managers. The latter provides a good illustration of the kinds of problems this can have for new management initiatives. Increasingly the personal career strategies of many managers mean that they remain in each job in each workplace for short periods only. In one sense the personal career strategy itself is probably based on long-term thinking, but the manager's personal hidden agenda for each particular job or at each particular workplace is more likely to be based on a short-term strategy. Whilst such managers may advocate greater commitment by employees to the company or organisation as part of an employee involvement programme, their personal agenda may bring their own commitment into doubt in the minds of non-management employees, and may act to undermine the credibility of the employee involvement programme itself. High turnover levels of management can act against any long-term strategy towards a new management initiatives programme, can result in markedly different levels of understanding and differences of approach towards new management initiatives by incoming managers, and may emphasise rapid change and 'management through stress' strategies as techniques for increased exploitation of employees' ability. The imposition of a new management initiatives programme in these circumstances may well be accompanied by increased cynicism of the workforce, whereas a change in workplace culture of the opposite kind is what is required by management if they are to succeed with a programme of new management initiatives.

iv. *Extensive use of numerical flexibility of labour, and associated low levels of investment in training* by employers in the UK are often linked to short-term cost-cutting strategies. The USA and the UK have gone further than other industrialised countries in deregulating the labour market through the extensive promotion of numerical flexibility of labour. However, UK employers in particular could pay a heavy price for this, not least because of the entrenched position many of them have taken on the issue. High labour turnover has been a consequence, which has discouraged employers from investing in training. A workforce poorly trained and poorly skilled compared with other EU countries may present a serious obstacle to the effective implementation of integrated and consistent programmes of new management initiatives by UK employers.[2] Also the high labour turnover which comes with extensive numerical flexibility of labour could conflict with employee involvement initiatives aimed at increasing the commitment of employees to the company. A further point is that poor investment levels in training may limit the potential for the implementation of effective functional flexibility of skilled labour.

v. However, there is a broader problem which employers in the UK may be faced with in their efforts to implement new management initiatives programmes. This is concerned with *a possible contradiction between the implications of employee involvement and the implications of other new management initiatives*. Employee involvement is portrayed by employers as a means of empowering employees. It is about changing workplace culture. It requires conciliatory, non-authoritarian styles of management in order to build teams and emphasise common interests between workers and management. However, can this be reconciled with the implications for the workplace of just-in-time, *kaizen*/continuous improvement, total quality methods, increased labour flexibility and the continuous demands for improved employee performance? Are not confrontational styles of management an inevitable consequence of a programme of management techniques which generally aim to increase the pace of work and the level of management demands on employees? Perhaps this depends on the extent to which new management initiative programmes are introduced by consent, whether this be through collective bargaining and negotiated settlements with trade unions or with the consent of employees in non-union workplaces. Alternatively, perhaps there are ways in which employers can actually introduce effective new management initiative programmes on the back of confrontation. Toyota and Nissan in Japan began their programmes with a fierce and decisive confrontation with the then independent trade unions, destroying their presence in those companies, and replacing them with company unions. In management terms, this was the successful basis for the implementation of a fully fledged programme of new management techniques and initiatives. However, long-term planning, fully integrated programmes of new techniques, and a revolution in management were other essential ingredients.

Such high risk 'full confrontation' strategies apart, there are perhaps three important categories to focus on: greenfield sites, non-union sites (which may or may not be greenfield) and established union workplaces. Greenfield sites with single union no-strike agreements allow the introduction of fully fledged new management initiative programmes by consent through a negotiated settlement with a trade union. In the case of greenfield non-union sites employers can claim the consent of the workforce simply by the fact that only workers who are enthusiastic about the company's programme and way of working are likely to be employed in the first place. In the case of non-union established workplaces, a well-planned and gradual employee involvement programme in the hands of competent and well-trained managers may well be able to win an impressive level of consent from the workforce for the programme of new management initiatives to follow, not least because of the absence in the workplace of an alternative source of ideas, of possibilities and of workplace culture, ie a trade union. The problem for management in reconciling the promise of empowering workers through employee involvement with other key elements of new management initiative programmes may be at its most difficult in established union workplaces.[3] Can management introduce such programmes on the basis of consent through a process of negotiated settlements with the recognised unions? Or will they go for direct and decisive confrontation with the unions with the aim of derecognition and destruction of the independent unions in the workplace? We may see some examples of the latter in the 1990s, but clearly it is a very high risk strategy for management and employers, and wherever they can succeed through a strategy of negotiated settlements with trade unions it seems more likely that they will opt for it.

A major problem for unions?

To turn to the issues facing the trade unions – are new management initiative programmes a major problem for them? Is not a strategy of negotiated settlement(s) a reasonable way forward for the unions in response to the new management initiatives? Several key points need to be considered in an attempt to answer these questions.

i. First, *what if unions adopted a position of total opposition to new management initiative programmes, and were successful in preventing their introduction in particular workplaces?* There is the argument that such employers, because of the absence of new management techniques, would find it increasingly difficult to compete in the sale of their goods or services, which in turn would result in job losses, and therefore would be contrary ultimately to the interests of employees and trade unionists themselves. This suggests that new management initiatives face trade unions with a dilemma similar to that associated with the introduction of new technology. In other words, trade unionists might argue that if they do not oppose the introduction of new management initiatives, they may lose jobs, lose influence in the workplace and lose bargaining power; if they do oppose it and are successful they may lose jobs or face closure in any case. The trade union policy solution in the case of new technology, *at least in theory,* has been to attempt to slow down and exercise some influence over the pace and way in which new technology has been introduced into the workplace. Does it follow, therefore, that the only real way forward for unions in the UK is to attempt to influence and negotiate the introduction of new management initiatives wherever possible, but starting from the premise that the introduction of such management programmes is inevitable and necessary if the business is to survive? The short answer is that this is probably not the case.

ii. This is because *there are serious doubts about whether* all *the new management initiatives being introduced by employers in the UK are actually necessary for business survival.* This comes back to the controversial arguments about numerical flexibility of labour. Would British companies really collapse if numerical flexibility of labour was discouraged and restricted? Companies in other EU countries do not seem to have faced serious problems as a result of avoiding extensive use of numerical labour flexibility. On another front, is BS5750 really so critical for quality assurance in workplaces? It is already apparent, rather after the event, that it is not suitable for some workplaces, and insufficient for others. What about employee involvement techniques? Are they all essential for business survival? Or are they more important specifically in terms of winning employee consent and establishing employee commitment to the other new management initiatives? If the answer to the last question is yes, then perhaps trade unions might effectively oppose certain employee involvement techniques where they can, in order to strengthen their hand in negotiating and exercising some degree of control or influence over the introduction of other new management initiatives.

Cutting across all these points may be the problem of the fundamental reduction in the bargaining power of the unions, as a result of high unemployment and prolonged periods of recession. This may have created a determination of employers to introduce new management initiatives regardless of trade union arguments, and unconcerned about the absence of an effective critical opposition in the workplace. It is perhaps worth noting that if the predominant trend is for the unilateral introduction of new initiatives by management, then the ultimate outcome may be a greater number of management errors and weaknesses in such programmes than would otherwise have been the case.

The general point which might be concluded from all this is that trade unions do not need to see new management initiative programmes as 'all or nothing' programmes if the business is to survive. There is no doubt that they can afford to adopt a critical approach towards new management initiatives and, whilst they need to understand the interrelationship between the different techniques, it is in their interest to try to negotiate on each initiative, step by step, so that they can develop a proper assessment of each, and of the real contribution each is likely to make to the success of the business. Unions may at times be able to beat management with their own arguments. It is also evident that management do not always know where they are going in respect of new management initiatives programmes in any case, and when they do, they do not always know how to get there. The fact that unions may not necessarily have sufficient power in the workplace to ensure that their arguments about new management initiatives are taken seriously by management, or to ensure new management initiatives are negotiated, may have some very serious implications for both unions and management. In the long term, management might even lose the most as a result.

iii. To move on to the third main issue, *is there scope for a general negotiated settlement between unions and employers in respect of new management initiatives?* A broad concept of negotiated settlement might refer to the idea of some kind of agreed framework or rules for the conduct of industrial relations as a whole in the country, along the lines of the general approach to industrial relations in the post-war period in the UK up until the 1970s. The concept could be used more specifically, for example to refer to the period of the Social Contract of the 1970s Labour governments. Regarding new management initiative programmes in the 1990s, it is difficult to imagine any kind of settlement being formally introduced by government or formally brought about through a national negotiating forum involving employer and union organisations as a whole. For this to have a chance of happening, a prerequisite might be a much more conducive, stable political environment, which swung the balance of power in favour of the trade unions.

Alternatively, could such a negotiated settlement evolve informally? It is difficult to see how this could occur except on the basis of an acceptance of the full validity of the post-Fordist concept. In other words, acceptance that we have already entered into a quite different set of economic, social and political conditions in the society in which industrial relations takes place. On the basis of this perspective, trade unions are seen to adopt a *permanently* weaker, and quite different, role from that of their pre-Thatcher position. They are seen as having no alternative but to move forward with the new management initiatives of increasingly competitive industry. It cannot be ignored that many academics and national trade union representatives have already adopted this or a similar perspective. In respect of the introduction of new management initiative programmes, a general negotiated settlement in these terms would be perceived as a 'realistic and necessary truce' between organised labour and employers. It would be a general informal agreement which would include a significant degree of trade union concession and compromise, and would emphasise apparent common ground between unions and employers regarding new management initiatives. Elements of this approach are evident in the policies of the AEEU.

Elements of such a general settlement might include wage agreements above the rate of inflation in exchange for far-reaching agreements on functional and temporal flexibility of labour. They might include joint initiatives on training as part of extensive functional flexibility agreements. Joint training initiatives might be agreed with unions in the workplace on pensions, health and safety and even mainstream union representatives courses, as an alternative to such training carried out by independent trade unions or the TUC. This could play an important role in the promotion of effective employee involvement. In return for such an approach to trade union education and training, union representatives might receive increased time for trade union duties. A general settlement between unions and employers could include trade union commitment to give up or radically restrict the right to strike, perhaps for a limited period, in exchange for significant wage settlements and extensive fringe benefits. The vulnerability of just-in-time to strike action might help to make this a particular target for employers. Any general settlement between unions and employers could also include a significant growth in the number of no-strike agreements on greenfield sites, whether these be of the Nissan type or some other variation.

If the post-Fordist concept proves to be a false explanation of developments, then the form which industrial relations might take in the coming years in the UK will be much more unpredictable, and there would appear to be too much instability in the system to talk about a negotiated settlement of a general nature between unions and employers in respect of new management initiatives. In any case, it is difficult to ignore a number of important factors contributing to levels of instability which make a general negotiated settlement of any lasting nature unlikely. These include the domestic and international economic climate, the difficulty of predicting the international patterns of recession, the rapid growth and difficulty of predicting the implications of nationalism, the ever-increasing intensification of international competition, and the continuing growth and somewhat unpredictable character of new management initiatives themselves. In spite of the collapse of Stalinism in Eastern Europe and the former Soviet states, it can still be argued that the use of Marxist methods of analysis have an important role to play in explaining such developments, and anticipating their future possible trends. And a rejection of the post-Fordist concept means that high unemployment may not necessarily be with us for ever, and that with any substantial upturn in the economy and substantial reduction in unemployment could come the re-emergence of strong trade unions. If this does occur then the situation would of course be transformed in terms of the negotiating position trade unions could take with regard to new management initiatives.

iv. A rather different issue to consider is *the extent to which trade unions might exploit management's weaknesses in relation to new management initiatives and techniques.* It was argued earlier that key management weaknesses included a management tendency to piecemeal or 'add-on' approaches, management's own resistance to change, predominance of short-term strategies, over-emphasis on numerical flexibility of labour, under-investment in training, and the questionable ability of management to meet the empowering promise of employee involvement. Just-in-time methods of production are also vulnerable to industrial action because of minimal stock levels. If these arguments are valid, then trade unions may have significant opportunities to influence, direct, control or resist new management initiatives, in spite of recession. If unions in the workplace not only have a clear grasp of what the various new management initiatives are about, and how they are related to each other, but also fully expose management weaknesses with regard to the new management initiatives, then workplace unions could command quite an effective negotiating position when faced with the introduction of new management initiatives. However, whilst unions might win *the argument* at this early stage, management's strong bargaining position created by recession and high unemployment may encourage management to plough on regardless. If such a programme runs into difficulty because of management weaknesses part way through its implementation, the crisis might be resolved in one of several ways. It may provide some good opportunities for the unions to renegotiate, win important concessions, redirect the programme and establish their influence over it in the future. Alternatively, it may result in an increasingly entrenched and defensive response by management, which may produce increasing disparity between management theory and practice in respect of the programme, and its eventual failure. Such circumstances of management vulnerability provide an important opportunity for unions to put across their case and increase their influence amongst both their members and management. Unfortunately, in some workplaces management are particularly skillful at disguising their own incompetences, and in these circumstances unions may still pay the price through job losses as a result.

If trade unions were to demonstrate a clear understanding of what the new management initiatives are all about, and where they are coming from, and present an array of well-organised arguments to management, it is quite feasible that unions could surpass the level of management expertise on the issue in many workplaces. It is even possible that in some workplaces trade unions could dominate the agenda with regard to this issue. However, the likelihood of unions operating in this way is influenced by questions of trade union policy, union strategy and tactics, the extent and level of debate within the unions about new management initiatives, and whether there is effective and extensive trade union education focused on the issues.

v. *Trade unions in the UK seem to have a number of significant weaknesses regarding their response to new management initiatives.* If the unions are to respond effectively to the new management initiatives, and protect trade union interests and independence, it can be argued that sooner or later they will need to address the following problems. First, there is evidence to suggest that a large gap remains between the demand for information about new management initiatives by union members and shop stewards in the workplace, and the output of information on the subject by trade union research and information departments and full-time officials. There is a small minority of unions which have produced members' guides to the issues, but these are mostly rather limited in scope, failing to cover the full range of new management initiatives and to explain the interrelationship between them.[4] Certainly unions face several problems in meeting the demand for such information, including severe pressures on resources as a result of declining membership, the speed and extent of new management initiatives, the complexity and breadth of the initiatives and how this information can be presented to members and shop stewards in a clear, accessible form. There may also be a problem of overcentralised, London-based research departments which may have difficulties in keeping in touch with the latest developments in the workplaces and the regions. Unions have increasingly published material about new management initiatives in the pages of their membership newspapers and journals, but this has mostly adopted a piecemeal approach to the issues.

Second, there is a general lack of debate within the trade union movement about the new management initiatives and how best to respond. This is not to say, for example, that motions have not been put to union conferences about specific new management initiatives, but again these have been mostly of a piecemeal nature.[5] There has been no serious attempt by most trade unions, and no serious attempt by the TUC, to organise a broad debate on the issues, and to pull together a coherent and comprehensive policy and strategy. This limited, piecemeal approach, by failing to explain and publicise the interrelationship between the various new management initiatives, has also had the effect of discouraging trade unionists from anticipating the next steps and implications of new management initiative programmes in their own workplaces. The lack of debate, and lack of information, has made them ill-equipped. It is not uncommon for shop stewards in industrial workplaces to allege that they know more about new management initiatives than the full-time staff of their own union.

The general lack of information and debate about new management initiatives and the absence of comprehensive policy statements and strategy, in many sections of the trade union movement, could be related to three broad positions. One is that the national leadership of some trade unions do not believe that the new management initiatives are a fundamental challenge to the authority, strength and independence of the trade unions. A second is that they do recognise that the new management initiatives are indeed such a challenge to the trade unions, but they are convinced that unions today do not have the strength to meet that challenge, and have no alternative but to respond in whatever pragmatic way they can from their unavoidable position of weakness. As a result, they believe no useful purpose would be served by encouraging public debate about the issues within the labour movement. A third explanation is that there is a predominance within the senior ranks of many trade unions of the view that unions will simply have to make the further major concessions implied by new management initiatives if British industry is to be regenerated, and whatever other differences there may be, such industrial regeneration is a common interest of both employers and trade unions. As a result, they believe no useful purpose would be served by encouraging public debate about the issues within the labour movement.

However, the limited debate and absence of comprehensive policy on the issues within the trade union movement may also be related to other, more sensitive, questions. It is difficult for the unions to debate and develop a comprehensive and effective strategy towards the new management initiatives and techniques without putting the spotlight on those sections of the trade union movement which are enthusiastic about joint union-management approaches to new management initiatives. This may risk provoking new divisions within the trade union movement, and open up the old wounds of the 1980s. It may provide new opportunities for the traditional left minority within the unions. In addition, how can the trade union movement focus considerable attention on new management initiatives, and the need for a comprehensive, assertive and effective policy and strategy towards them, without questioning the validity of Labour Party policy on these issues? To be effective, debate within the trade union movement about new management initiatives, and resultant policy and strategy, needs to be wide-ranging. Such a debate may indeed be a cause of concern for the Labour Party because it could call into question its established policy of building business confidence and a partnership with industry. It may also unnerve the leadership of a number of large trade unions, not only because of its possible implications for the Labour Party, but also because of the potentially provocative nature of such a debate and its potentially divisive implications within the trade union movement.

The expulsion of the EETPU and the threatened departure of the AEU from the TUC was a disturbing experience for the trade union movement in the 1980s. The EETPU's handling of single union no-strike deals called into question the essential authority of the TUC. The readmittance of the EETPU into the TUC, as a section of the AEEU with which it merged, can be interpreted as an important milestone in the declining authority of the TUC. The position that the TUC leadership appeared to take throughout the dispute was that it could not afford to lose the affiliation of both the EETPU and the AEU, and in the process risk the establishment of an alternative trade union centre to the TUC. These events may have contributed to a new view of the role of the TUC on the part of the majority of the large unions, and an acceptance that the policies and strategies of individual affiliated unions may become increasingly diverse. If this is the case, then the prospects of a co-ordinated, comprehensive debate about the new management initiatives, and resultant policy and strategy guidelines for the trade union movement as a whole are not encouraging. Instead very considerable variation in policy and practice of trade unions towards new management initiatives may emerge.

Some unions, TUC-affiliated or otherwise, may follow the AEEU model of joint union-management approaches to the new management initiatives and techniques. Other unions may make major concessions to management in respect of the new initiatives unnecessarily, and effectively by default, because of their failure to develop policy and strategy guidelines for their local negotiators, and to prepare them for the challenge presented by management. In due course, yet other unions may develop co-ordinated, comprehensive policies and strategies to guide local negotiators and protect trade union independence, in spite of the difficulties. It is feasible that one or two unions in each sector could become the model for other unions to follow in a struggle to defend trade union independence. Rather than co-ordination of strategy emerging through the TUC, a possible development might be an increasing exchange between particular unions of such model agreements, model policy and strategy guidelines on new management initiatives, through a growing web of inter-union relationships and alliances.

For such a trade union response to new management techniques to emerge, there would need to be a major shift in the dominant perspective of the labour movement, not least in the political outlook of the leadership. To defend and advance the interests of independent trade unionism, faced with the threat of new management techniques, what is required is a recognition of the centrality of conflict in the workplace. An effective analysis of the new management techniques needs to be theoretically founded on such an approach.

In spite of the powerful shift to the right in recent years, the labour movement has retained the capacity to organise a response which advances the interests of independent trade unionism. This book is an attempt to contribute to both the practical and theoretical dimensions of such a response.

Notes

1 For an outline of the perspective adopted see A. Ferner and R. Hyman, *Industrial Relations in the New Europe*, Blackwell, 1992, ppxviii-xix; also R. Hyman, 'Plus ca change? The Theory of Production and the Production of Theory', A. Pollert (ed), *Farewell to Flexibility?*, Blackwell, 1991.
2 S. Lewis, 'Adding Value to Workers', *Investors Chronicle*, 30.7.93, p16.

3   It is interesting to consider this issue in relation to employee participation as well as employee involvement.

4   This is not to deny the value to union members of some union pamphlets on the subject. Of those produced by trade unions, the following are useful: Ian Linn/NUCPS, *Employers' Offensive – Human Resource Management and Employee Communications*, 1992; TGWU, *Employee Involvement and Quality Circles*, 1989 edit.; Ian Linn/Northern College/TGWU Region 10, *Single Union Deals*, 1986. Other useful labour movement publications include: Tyne and Wear County Association of Trades Councils, *Nissan and Single Trade Union Agreements*, 1988; G.Coyne and H.Williamson, *New Union Strategies – Trade Union Responses to New Management Techniques*, Centre for Alternative Industrial and Technological Systems (CAITS) and Merseyside Trade Union, Community and Unemployed Resource Centre, 1991; Mike George and Hugo Levie, *Japanese Competition and the British Workplace*, CAITS, 1984; CAITS, *Flexibility – Who Needs It?*, 1986.

5   The TGWU have taken some initiatives which are contrary to this trend. An important debate on new management techniques took place at the TGWU Biennial Delegate Conference 1993, and a composite motion was carried on the subject (TGWU, *Record*, August 1993, p9).

Index

TRADE UNIONS IN THE EUROPEAN UNION
A Handbook

by Wolfgang Lecher
translated by Pete Burgess

Trade Unions in the European Union is a thorough and up-to-date guide to the different forms of employee representation in the countries of the European Union, as well as to the different legal, political and economic conditions in which trade unions operate.

Containing a wealth of statistical and factual information, including over 40 tables and the relevant parts of the famous Social Chapter, **Trade Unions in the European Union** is the essential reference work for all those who work in the areas of industrial relations, labour law and human resource management.

ISBN 0 85315 766 9
£14.99 paperback

Available from all good bookshops or direct from

Lawrence & Wishart Ltd
144a Old South Lambeth Road
London SW8 1XX

Tel 071-820 9281
Fax 071-587 0469